HOW TO BE A GREAT BOSS

Other Books by Gino Wickman

Traction
Decide!
Get a Grip, with Mike Paton
Rocket Fuel, with Mark C. Winters

HOW
TO BE A
GREAT
BOSS

GINO WICKMAN
AND RENÉ BOER

BenBella Books, Inc.
Dallas, TX

BenBella Books, Inc.
10440 N. Central Expy., Suite 800 | Dallas, TX 75231
www.benbellabooks.com | Send feedback to feedback@benbellabooks.com

Printed in the United States of America
10 9 8 7 6 5 4 3 2 1

Library of Congress Cataloging-in-Publication Data
is available upon request.
ISBN-13: 978-1-942952-84-8 | e-ISBN: 978-1-942952-85-5

Editing by Glenn Yeffeth
Copyediting by James Fraleigh
Proofreading by Brittney Martinez and Cape Cod Compositors, Inc.
Text design and composition by Silver Feather Design
Graphic design by Drew Robinson Spork Design
Front cover design by Emily Weigel, Faceout Studio
Jacket design by Sarah Dombrowsky
Printed by Lake Book Manufacturing

Distributed by Perseus Distribution www.perseusdistribution.com
To place orders through Perseus Distribution:
Tel: (800) 343-4499 | Fax: (800) 351-5073
E-mail: orderentry@perseusbooks.com

Special discounts for bulk sales (minimum of 25 copies) are available.
Please contact Aida Herrera at aida@benbellabooks.com.

To my 135 clients. The 1,700 full-day sessions we have done together were the proving ground for every word in this book.
—GINO WICKMAN

To my supportive, resilient, and wonderful wife, Judy. Thank you for always being there for me. I love you very much.
—RENÉ BOER

CONTENTS

WHY THE WORD "BOSS"?

Consider this for a minute: no matter what title is on your business card, be it foreman, supervisor, manager, director, vice president, president, or chief executive officer, the people who report to you call you their *boss*.

The word "boss" comes from the Dutch word "baas," originally a term of respect used to address a person in charge. We use "boss" purposely because that is what you are—someone in charge, who leads and manages people. If you are ever in doubt, please come back to this definition.

We urge you to wear the title "boss" with pride. You're in charge. Be in charge. Don't be apologetic or tiptoe around it. Don't give in to all the politically correct and watered-down titles such as "team leader," "coach," or "people champion." These terms certainly describe what a great boss is and does; they're just not all-encompassing titles. Take pride in the responsibility, but don't become arrogant or take the title "boss" for granted.

Never use the phrase "I'm the boss" in an overbearing or entitled manner. No one respects people like that. Instead, they whisper behind the backs of bosses who are so stuck on themselves that they take their authority and responsibility lightly.

Walk through the offices or visit the production floors of great companies and you're likely to find engaged employees who are well led by great bosses. Those bosses create an environment where people show up every day because they want to be there, not because they have to.

So, if you're a leader or manager of people and you aspire to be a great boss, this book is written for you. You need only keep an open mind and commit to becoming great. We'll provide you with the tools to help you get there.

CHAPTER 1

being a great boss

"If we treat people as they ought to be, we help them become what they are capable of becoming."

—GOETHE

WHAT IF EVERY DAY YOUR PEOPLE brought their "A game" to work? Do you believe that is even possible?

In the next 154 pages we intend to show that it *is* possible, and we will teach you the tools that will transform how well your people perform for you. You will discover how to:

- effectively delegate work and free yourself up to truly lead and manage,

- assess your team and surround yourself with Great People,

- apply five leadership practices and five management practices of all great bosses,
- communicate powerfully with each of your employees, and
- deal with employees that don't meet your expectations.

This book is different from any other leadership or management book you've ever read—and literally tens of thousands of them have been written. What makes it different is its practical application and immediate impact. It offers no theory. Instead, it offers a straightforward game plan to help you become a great leader and manager. We can say that because every word and tool in this book have been tested and proven by thousands of leaders and managers whose influence and results are undeniable.

In the last twenty years we have personally worked with the leadership teams of more than 180 companies and more than 2,000 leaders and managers. In addition, our organization, EOS Worldwide, has 150 EOS Implementers around the world who have taught these tools to another 2,500 companies and more than 25,000 leaders and managers. Because we have tackled day-in, day-out problems with so many bosses, we know what works and what does not.

Gino's first book, *Traction*, which has sold hundreds of thousands of copies, uncovered a vital need in the small business world: a need for a simple, real-world guide to help the leaders and managers of entrepreneurial companies become great bosses. That compelled us to write this book and provide that simple formula. Anyone with direct reports who is seeking a practical, proven way to excel at what they do can follow these steps to bring out the best in their people.

This book is for you if:

- you are a leader, manager, or supervisor of people in a privately held, 10- to 250-person entrepreneurial company; or

- you want to get the most out of your people and seek a simple, effective, and impactful way to become a great boss.

This book is also written to help the "not-so-good bosses" get out of the way—to help them acknowledge that they lack the basic understanding, desire, and capacity to develop the skills that will make them great.

We have learned that to get the most from your people— to have a highly motivated workforce—you, in your role as boss, must create an environment where your people will thrive. Matthew Kelly, in his book *Off Balance: Getting Beyond the Work-Life Balance Myth to Personal and Professional Satisfaction*, points out that highly motivated employees enjoy both personal and professional satisfaction from what they do. "They work hard ... they enjoy the people they work with; they feel respected by their boss; they feel their work is making a contribution to customers' lives; they find the challenge of their work matches their abilities; and they know why they go to work each day."

This may be apparent to you already, but what is surprising is this: Kelly, in his efforts to find a link between "work-life balance" and a highly engaged workforce, interviewed well-respected people at dozens of the world's best companies. He asked these companies if he could interview people who they thought best exemplified work-life balance. What he discovered after interviewing these people was that they actually worked an average of nine hours *more* per week than their counterparts did. They valued job satisfaction over work-life balance. So, when you focus your efforts to improve your people's satisfaction level with their jobs, versus the number of hours they work, think of the upside.

Here's something else we've learned after we surveyed our clients at EOS Worldwide. When asked why they engaged us, 82.4 percent reported they were not getting enough out of their people; they weren't on the same page, working together to win. In fact, "people issues" are one of the most common frustrations shared by bosses—not sales, not profit . . . people! However, keep this in mind: *as frustrated as you might be with your people, the fact is, they are your number one competitive advantage.*

Think about that for a minute. You may hold patents, own proprietary technology, and have tremendous brand awareness, but in the end, it all boils down to people. So, for better or worse, the people you employ or who report directly to you are your only real differentiator.

Competitors can steal your ideas and copy your products. After all, they essentially do what you do. They can even steal your playbook—how you do what you do. But it doesn't matter because in the end, being a great boss comes down to execution—doing what you do better than the competition. Here is a great example. During the 1960s, opponents of the Green Bay Packers, who won two Super Bowls and five NFL Championships during that decade, had seen Vince Lombardi's famous "Power Sweep" so many times that they not only knew the play inside and out, they also knew when it was coming. But they still couldn't stop it. Lombardi was that good at leading his players to become that good at running that play.

The advantage of being a boss like Lombardi is that you have the opportunity to surround yourself with people who you want to work with and who want to succeed. You have the responsibility to hire them and fire them. If you're not satisfied with the performance of the people reporting to you, you have to accept the responsibility of doing something about it. However, before you fire anyone, you must ask yourself, "Have I done everything possible to make them successful? Have I failed them in any way?" Make sure you've done your part.

As we've mentioned, the tools we teach in this book are simple; they have to be, because the journey to become a great boss is not easy. People often confuse "simple" and "easy." The definition of "simple" is *not elaborate, not complicated, easy to understand.* The definition of "easy" is *not hard or difficult; requiring no great effort; free from pain, discomfort or care.*

The tools and exercises that comprise this "how to" guide have been honed while working hands-on with thousands of bosses. In each chapter we share stories from every type of boss—owners, leadership team members, managers, and supervisors—to show you that these tools truly work for bosses at any level. They will help you lead, manage, and retain the sort of employees we call Great People. And the more Great People you surround yourself with, the more Great People you will attract to your organization. These Great People will free you from the day-to-day grind that has kept you from getting the most from your business and living a more fulfilling life. If we've piqued your interest, read on.

STATE OF THE AMERICAN WORKFORCE

Since 2000, the Gallup Organization has been conducting an annual survey of American workers. The results haven't changed much year to year and reveal that only 31.5 percent of full-time American workers are "engaged" at their jobs. These employees show up early, leave late, come up with creative solutions, attract and retain customers, and bring energy to the workplace. Jim Clifton, Gallup's CEO, asserts that this group more than likely works for a great boss.

However, Gallup reports that 17.5 percent of American workers are "actively disengaged" at work. This group likely works for a boss that makes them miserable, and as a result, they spread their discontent throughout the organization. These employees are more likely to steal from their employer, miss days at work, and drive customers away.

Sadly, the survey shows that the remaining 51 percent of American workers are "not engaged" at work! These employees meet the minimum requirements, but they don't view their jobs as a major component of their daily lives. They're flying just under the radar while collecting their paycheck. It's been estimated that their lost productivity costs American businesses a staggering $500 billion annually.

Clifton goes on to state that the single most important decision that business owners make is deciding whom to hire or promote to management positions. Choosing the right people propels their companies forward, while the wrong people hold them back. Additionally, a 2015 Harris Poll revealed that 39 percent of employees have no idea of their company's goals and objectives, 47 percent are unfamiliar with the state of their company's performance, and 44 percent don't understand how the role they play helps the organization meet its goals.

Think about the implications for your organization. Gallup suggests that only a third of your employees are actually driving your results. If everyone were actively engaged at work, what results could you achieve?

Whether your results are better or worse than those revealed by these polls, you can see that significant opportunity may well exist in your organization. Are you willing to take responsibility for all the issues that have caused employees to disengage? For example, if you are constantly frustrated with people who don't meet your expectations, but you don't explain your expectations, you may be part of the problem. Acknowledging and taking responsibility for poor employee performance and engagement is the first step. Poor bosses don't grasp this and will blame factors "beyond their control." Great bosses will rise to the challenge. Which boss are you?

We're facing a crisis that is not just measured by a lack of opportunity for the workforce, but also by the lack of enthusiasm that the workforce has for their jobs. We're losing our competitive advantage. You cannot expect to meet your goals with half your team sitting on the bench—and 17.5 percent actually heckling you. You need an engaged, raring-to-go workforce. Your choices are to lead, follow, or get out of the way. You must decide. And remember, choosing not to be a great boss is okay. Just get out of the way and be willing to follow.

So, do your people truly matter to you? Do you view them as your number one competitive advantage? Are you excited about building a team of highly motivated employees and getting the most from them? If so, then get ready to answer the question that starts the next chapter.

CHAPTER 2

do you have what it takes?

"Most people work just hard enough not to get fired and get paid just enough money not to quit."

—George Carlin

YOU CAN REACT in one of two ways to comedian George Carlin's joke. The not-so-great bosses laugh and nod their heads, accepting his words as the status quo. They're often heard saying, "Good people are so hard to find." Or, "I don't pass out many compliments because when I do, they expect a raise." Or, "Why invest in training when they'll leave us in a heartbeat for more money?"

By contrast, great bosses see beyond the intended humor and realize that the problem isn't with the people, it's with the not-so-good bosses who lead those people. They don't accept this sad state of affairs. They're willing to challenge the status quo. They're often heard saying, "I've got a great team of people and I feel privileged to lead them" and "My people keep me on my toes and make me better."

A boss that exemplifies this is Trevor Moses of imageOne, a managed print provider. He believes that, as a boss, one of his responsibilities is to develop his people and improve their skills. This makes them more upwardly mobile within his organization, and in the highly unlikely event that his company should close its doors, more marketable when they look for a job immediately afterward.

So, whether you find Carlin's humor funny or not, you must take responsibility for your people as Moses does and be willing to do something about it.

Great bosses earn the respect of those they lead; they don't take it for granted. Sadly, too many bosses don't get it. They think their title empowers them with unquestioned authority to act in whatever manner they deem necessary. These bosses view themselves as kings and queens of their realm. In their minds they rule supreme. This line of destructive thinking didn't play out well for France's King Louis XVI. In 1793, after his subjects rose up in revolt, they shortened his inflated ego by about a foot—a head, actually.

In this chapter, we ask you to evaluate whether you're truly up for the challenge of being a great boss. We will explain that to fill that role, you must:

1. **Get it**—have the aptitude, natural ability, and thorough understanding of the ins and outs of the job;

2. **Want it**—sincerely desire the role;

3. Have the **Capacity to do it**—possess the emotional, intellectual, physical, and time capacity to do the job.

The first two assets—"get it" *and* "want it" are essential for becoming a great boss. No one can help you "get it" or "want it." Either you have these two things or you do not. The third asset—"capacity to do it"—can be acquired if you are willing to invest the time and effort to excel in the role.

UNDERSTANDING "GET IT"

You've probably worked with people who, despite extensive training, coaching, and time in the position, didn't have a thorough grasp of their role, the organization's systems, pace, or culture, or the ins and outs of the job—they simply didn't get it.

To be a great boss, you must honestly ask yourself if you truly *get it*—that you thoroughly grasp the job. You must comprehend it so well that there is no question in your own mind or those of your peers and direct reports.

Ken Robinson, in his book, *The Element: How Finding Your Passion Changes Everything*, defines "get it" as follows: "Get it is aptitude; or the natural ability for something. An intuitive feel or grasp of what the job is, how it works and how to do it. Natural feel: biochemistry."

One great boss demonstrated that he had the intuitive feel for the job when, as general manager, he was deployed by a national retailer to turn around one of its worst-performing stores. After careful analysis, the company had decided to close the worst of their outlets. On that list was a store that had them baffled. Although it was located in an area with plenty of traffic and great visibility, it continually lagged behind other stores in the system.

In a last-ditch effort to turn things around, the company placed this great boss, a manager who "gets it," in charge of the store. Several weeks later, the store's sales were making steady upward progress, which delayed the decision to close it. Within a few months, the store was one of the top performers in the system—amazingly, with very little turnover and no additional cost.

When asked how he had accomplished the feat, the manager replied that he simply asked each employee whether he or she was a "box person" or a "people person." He explained that a box person is well organized and great at keeping things in their place, whereas a people person enjoys engaging customers and meeting their needs. He then assigned people in each group appropriately, allowing them to leverage their individual strengths.

This is a good example of a boss who truly "gets it." That natural aptitude and ability is fundamental to being a boss. No public relations or marketing efforts in the world would have made a difference in keeping that store open. It required someone who "got" how to lead and manage people in a big box retail store.

Now, with this story in mind, are your actions as a boss showing others that you truly get it? For instance, do you use the same approach to motivate every employee, or do you have a deeper understanding and appreciation of them as individuals? Do you have that instinctive feel for rallying everyone according to the way they work best? Imagine how your employees would describe you to their friends or fellow workers. What would they say?

UNDERSTANDING "WANT IT"

Next, you must ask yourself if you truly *want it*—that you genuinely desire the job of being a great boss. No one talked you into it or begged you to take it. No one promised you a raise, a bonus, or a company car to entice you. You might have a bad day or two—that's normal—but the challenges and obstacles energize you. You enjoy overcoming those obstacles. They don't wear you down.

One of our clients described a former boss who would occasionally ask midlevel managers who he suspected didn't want it, "Do you have the fire in your belly to lead?" In almost every case that person would answer yes. He followed that question with this statement: "You are *telling* me you want to lead, but you're not *showing* me." This served as a wake-up call for those managers, a friendly tap on the shoulder to remind them that actions needed to follow words.

John Eadie, founding partner of Covenant Multifamily Offices in San Antonio, Texas, says this about wanting it: "I have had the benefit of great teaching and training throughout my career, but I've come to realize that even when people receive great training and have great mentors, unless they really 'want it,' those things likely will not stick. It's gratifying to work with people who truly want it and are willing to put in the effort necessary to achieve it."

So, do you have the "fire in your belly" for the trials and tribulations of being a great boss? Do your actions show others that you truly want it? As an example, are you willing to go the extra mile to get a project completed on time, or do you leave work early regardless of how it affects your team or customers? Again, imagine how your employees would describe you to their friends or fellow workers. What would they say?

The fact is that many bosses really don't get it or want it—yet both are crucial. Think about it: you could absolutely "get" the role of being a boss but just not "want it." Or, you could "want it" with all your heart and soul but not "get it." In either scenario you'll never be a great boss. You must "get it" *and* "want it."

Assuming that you get it and you want it, the next question is, "Do you have the capacity to do it?"

UNDERSTANDING "CAPACITY TO DO IT"

While not getting it or wanting it are deal killers, some problems of capacity can be solved. If you lack any of the aspects of capacity described next but are willing to invest the time, resources, and energy to gain them, you can become a great boss.

THE FOUR
TYPES OF CAPACITY

If you're fortunate, you've worked for a great boss in the past or you're working for one now, one who probably possesses the four types of capacity to do a great job. You therefore have a role model you can emulate. Now, here's the question to ask yourself: "Do I have the emotional, intellectual, physical, and time capacity to be a great boss?" Let's take them one at a time:

1. Emotional Capacity

The *heart* to feel what others are feeling, the ability to walk a mile in their shoes, to be open and honest with yourself and others, a willingness to be real and connect with others, to be humbly confident, and to be self-aware enough to know how you are influencing people.

2. Intellectual Capacity

The *brains* to do critical thinking, solve complex problems, predict, prioritize, and plan, along with the ability to conceptualize, strategize, and systematize how best to do things while orchestrating human resources. F. Scott Fitzgerald described intelligence as "the ability to hold two opposed ideas in the mind at the same time, and still retain the ability to function."

3. Physical Capacity

The *stamina*, energy, and tenacity to do what it takes to finish what you start, to "pour it on" when necessary, to devote the time and effort to master your craft, to do the work, and to get your hands dirty when necessary.

4. Time Capacity

The *self-discipline* to use your time effectively, to avoid the tyranny of urgency, to structure, prioritize, organize, and delegate in a way that frees up and optimizes the most precious resource of all—your time.

––––––––––

If you've been in the workforce for any length of time, you've probably worked for a not-so-good boss. You've witnessed firsthand how a boss who lacks any of the four types of capacity can harm a department or an entire organization. Here are some examples:

Low Emotional Capacity

These bosses are usually oblivious to the signals their subordinates are sending them about how their behavior affects others. At best, they make a superficial connection with their people. They're not honest with themselves and lack the self-confidence to be open and honest enough to say, "I don't know, I need your help, I made a mistake." They'll take credit for success but avoid accepting responsibility when things go wrong.

Low Intellectual Capacity

These bosses usually lack the ability to visualize an outcome before taking a course of action. They tend to set objectives without anticipating the resources needed to meet those goals. They lack mental agility, overanalyzing some things and oversimplifying others.

Low Physical Capacity

These bosses lack the stamina and energy necessary to see tasks to completion. They rarely leave the office to inspect what they expect. They're unable or unwilling to do the hard work, to get their hands dirty, or to pitch in when needed.

Low Time Capacity

These bosses are usually a whirling dervish of activity, robbing time from others while using theirs to pursue things that are "in the moment." They expect others to drop what they're doing to help them get caught up. They're usually late for meetings, behind schedule, overwhelmed, and afraid or incapable of letting go.

Although these criticisms sound a bit harsh, they probably fit bosses you know. To excel as a great boss, you must possess all four types of capacity. If you don't, you must first take stock of yourself to acknowledge anything you need to work on. More than that, you must commit to exerting the considerable effort necessary to develop a capacity that you don't already possess.

The bosses that don't get it, want it, or have the capacity to do it are often the root cause of organizational dysfunction and their company's poor performance. They think, "If those knuckleheads didn't bang on my door all the time, I'd love being a boss!" Don't blame the guys on the loading dock, or the salespeople, or the technicians. Bad bosses drive their best employees and eventually their best customers away. They feel threatened by people smarter, more capable, or more motivated than them. They run from conflict, unwilling to confront real issues or make unpopular decisions. They're quick to point out flaws in others while ignoring their own.

If, after reading this chapter, you realize that you don't get it, want it, or have the capacity to fill the role of boss, do yourself a favor and step down. Do something that truly inspires you. Life is too short to spend it doing something that makes you miserable and leaves you feeling unfulfilled and continually frustrated. Being a bad boss does not make you a bad person, just a bad boss. To paraphrase the Wizard of Oz when Dorothy called him a bad man: "Oh, no, my dear; I'm really a very good man, I'm just a very bad Wizard."

If this describes you, don't despair. The fact is you do have a God-given skill set. It's just not as a boss. You owe it to yourself to discover your unique skill set and then pursue it with all your heart.

On the other hand, if you realize that you haven't been a great boss, but you are ready, willing, and able to become one, there's still hope. Paraphrasing Pogo: "You have met the enemy and he is you." It's time to learn about a powerful tool that will help you get there.

CHAPTER 3

delegate and elevate™

"The average person puts only 25% of his energy and ability into his work. The world takes off its hat to those who put in more than 50% of their capacity, and stands on its head for those few and far between souls who devote 100%."

—Andrew Carnegie

IF YOU'RE LIKE MANY BOSSES that we've worked with, you are frustrated by a lack of time to do your job well. In this chapter we will teach you the ultimate time management tool, Delegate and Elevate™, to help you clarify and identify the activities that you must delegate to others in order to free up your time capacity to be a great boss.

Completing the Delegate and Elevate exercise helps you discover whether you truly want to do boss-related activities focused on leading and managing people. It also shows you how to look at the activities you find yourself doing over the course of a week or month. Further, it explores how much you enjoy them and your competence in doing them. This will help you "discover" those activities that energize you and those you should delegate to others. Remember, to become a great boss, you need enough time. This tool will put your true gifts in perspective so you can focus your energy and time on your strengths. After all, no one has the ability or time to do everything, and the sooner you delegate, the better your department will run.

The Delegate and Elevate exercise is a five-step process that should not be hurried. We ask you to be thorough with each step. They are as follows:

Step 1

List all of the business-related activities that you do during the course of a day, week, and month. Write them down in a journal or a notebook. This list may take several hours to compile over a period of a week or longer, so do not rush it. Be patient and detailed.

Step 2

After completing your list of business-related activities, compare it to the sample of boss-related activities provided on page 25 in Diagram 1. Add any activities that you overlooked to your list. *Please note that in the third column of*

Diagram 1, we have listed some boss-related activities that are specific to dealing with direct reports.

Step 3

When you're satisfied that you have a complete list of all your activities, turn to Diagram 2 and place each activity into one of the four quadrants. Please be completely honest with yourself as you add them to the appropriate quadrant.

Step 4

In the four quadrants, examine where you placed the activities that Diagram 1 indicates are boss related and specific to dealing with direct reports. (To make this easier, mark them with a highlighter.) A minimum of 80 percent of those activities from the boss-related list in the third column of Diagram 1 should be in the top two quadrants, along with most of the items in the first and second columns.

If most of them are in the top two quadrants, you probably have what it takes (the capacity) to be a great boss. If not, you may find more satisfaction and fulfillment in applying your expertise and technical skill in a role that doesn't require you to lead and manage others.

Step 5

If you cannot accomplish all of the business activities you listed in the time you have, then you have a time-capacity issue. You need to "delegate and elevate" the activities in the bottom two quadrants that are occupying too much of your time. We will address exactly how to do this in the next few pages.

SAMPLE LIST OF BOSS-RELATED ACTIVITIES

Activities dealing with technical skill, experience and expertise		Activities dealing with direct reports
Achieving goals	Being in meetings	Recognizing & rewarding
Brainstorming	Building systems	Performance reviews
Developing processes	Financial analysis	Coaching subordinates
Forecasting	Strategic planning	Directing people
Leading innovation	Meeting deadlines	Training
Managing workflow	Assigning tasks	Mediating disputes
Networking	Making presentations	Listening
Paying bills	Booking travel	Managing conflict
Problem solving	Managing projects	Mentoring
Purchasing	Vendor relations	Facilitating meetings
Raising capital	Customer relations	Firing people
Researching	Reporting	Delegating
Reviewing legal docs	Reviewing invoices	
Scheduling meetings	Responding to emails	
Signing checks	Negotiating	
Software stuff	Hardware stuff	
Sourcing candidates	Organizing	
Speaking to groups	Blogs, White Papers	
Writing emails	Reading trade publications	
Building key relationships	Strategic initiatives	
Community relations	Dealing with the press	

Note: Items in **Bold** are boss-related activities that are specific to **dealing with direct reports**.

Diagram 1

DELEGATE AND ELEVATE™

1) Love Doing It and Great at Doing It	2) Like Doing It and Good at Doing It
3) Don't Like Doing It and Good at Doing It	4) Don't Like Doing It and Not Good at Doing It

Diagram 2

Delegate and Elevate™ Quadrants

Quadrant 1 - "Love/Great" activities are those that you've mastered, that you love doing, that give you energy and a sense of fulfillment.

Quadrant 2 - "Like/Good" activities are those that you can do with minimal effort and that give you enjoyment and satisfaction.

Quadrant 3 - "Don't Like/Good" activities are those that you are good at doing—you have learned to do them well through repetition and necessity—but that don't give you real satisfaction or a sense of fulfillment.

Quadrant 4 - "Don't Like/Not Good" activities are most likely outside your area of expertise and leave you feeling inadequate and frustrated.

We hope that this exercise has been an eye-opener for you, allowing you to reflect on activities that you do on a regular basis, probably with little thought as to why you do them or how much you really enjoy doing them. You have fallen into a groove and it has become a routine. That's natural. However, if you're not careful, a routine can become a rut.

Let's compare the bolded *and* non-bolded business-related activities in Diagram 1. If you are a person who loves and is great at doing the bolded items (people-related skills) but haven't mastered the non-bolded items (technical skills), you may be a great people person. Those skills alone, however, are not enough to make you a great boss.

Conversely, if you are someone who loves and is great at doing the non-bolded items (technical skills) but dreads doing the ones in bold (people-related skills), you may be technically competent and a great manager of things—just not people. Technical skills alone won't make you a great boss, either.

Take a close look at the top two quadrants. Where did you place the "boss-related activities" (the ones in bold from Diagram 1 or the ones you highlighted) that are specific to dealing with direct reports? Are most of those activities in the top two quadrants? We hope that they are. If not, take heart. Great bosses aren't born; they develop. You may have placed activities that are specific to dealing with direct reports in the bottom two quadrants because you have failed at doing them well in the past. The reasons for why you failed may be unrelated to your capacity to be a great boss. Like you, many bosses find themselves consumed by the activities that they find themselves doing each day. If you're willing to develop the skills to become a great boss and delegate the rest, there's hope. If not, don't kid yourself. You'll struggle to fulfill the role of a great boss and you'll continue to frustrate yourself and those you're trying to lead. Life is too short to be doing things that you don't get, want, or have the capacity to do.

You don't always have the luxury of delegating all the things that you do. However, to leverage your emotional, intellectual, physical, and *time* capacity to do the job, you must develop a plan to delegate items in the bottom two quadrants. You can't be great at everything, and you'll never have the time to become a great boss if you don't let go of the things that bog you down. Despite working long hours, many bosses complain that they still don't have enough time to get everything done. That reminds us of a quip attributed to Robert Frost: "By working faithfully eight hours a day you may eventually get to be boss and work twelve hours a day." As a bonus, when you spend most of your time doing activities that you placed in the top two quadrants—the activities that you love to do and are great at doing—more than likely time seems to fly.

Time is the most precious resource great bosses have. You should be spending yours on the most important matters in your department. If you're running off to mail a package or to pick up office supplies, you're wasting precious time. Delegate it! There are only twenty-four hours in a day, so use them wisely.

Now, think of Diagram 3 on the next page as your seat in the organization and as an illustration of your "time capacity" for that seat. Then think of the roles that you must fulfill as a boss. Please know that you determine your time capacity—the hours to effectively do the job. For some, it's forty hours per week. For others it may be sixty. You decide. Whatever you choose—that's your time capacity. People who work at 120 percent of their time capacity are bound for disaster. You won't be an effective boss with a high level of job satisfaction and fulfillment if you're continually operating beyond your time capacity. You'll burn out or suffer serious health issues.

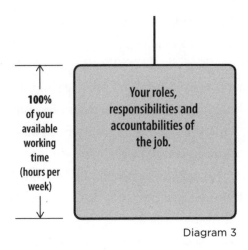

Diagram 3

If you decide that fifty hours per week is your magic number, then that is your 100 percent. If you then take sixty hours per week to get the job done, you are working at 120 percent capacity. It is time for you to delegate 20 percent (ten hours) of what you are doing to get back to 100 percent. The activities you should delegate should come from the bottom two quadrants, freeing you up to spend time in the top two quadrants. Ideally, you should delegate additional activities to get down to 90 percent capacity. This will proactively free up extra capacity to prepare you for growth. At the very least, it will give you extra time to handle the emergencies that inevitably come up every week.

By delegating the activities in the bottom two quadrants, you're actually doing yourself and your team a big favor. You are elevating yourself to do what you love to do and what you do well. You therefore make yourself more valuable to the organization, not to mention being happier and more energetic.

You are doing your team a favor for several reasons. First, you are freeing up more of your time to spend with them, ensuring they feel more valued. You are giving them more responsibility and more autonomy. You'll stop being a bottleneck to those that report to you. Best of all, your people may be more competent than you are at doing the things that you've delegated to them. For instance, if you are not so great at community relations but it's important to your company, determine who on your team would enjoy doing it and be good at doing it. Then delegate it to them.

Debra Hutson, a manager for a distribution company in Texas, did just that with her entire department. She called it "Help Debra Day." After sharing her Delegate and Elevate self-assessment with her team, she discovered that many activities that she had placed in the bottom two quadrants were actually activities that a few people on her team loved to do. She delegated those activities and improved both her time capacity and her department's effectiveness.

Oftentimes, bosses resort to the familiar when they're under stress. "If I do it, I know the thing will get done right" goes that line of thinking. They find themselves doing what they've hired others to do. This frustrates some of their direct reports while enabling others to avoid accountability. This behavior has many negative consequences, not the least of which is lost productivity and the inability to focus on the activities that are really the best use of their time.

We recognize that delegating is simple in theory but not easy in practice. Plus, you may be resistant to letting go. Here's a list of the most common reasons bosses give for not delegating:

1. Being good at these activities got me promoted in the first place.

2. I have no one to delegate to.

3. It takes too much time for me to train someone.

4. I find that it's faster and easier to do it myself.

5. I wouldn't ask anyone to do anything I wouldn't do myself.

6. No one can do it as well as me.

7. It's too complicated to explain it to them.

8. I spend too much time fixing their mistakes.

We categorize these reasons as the "personal head trash" that prevents people from becoming great bosses.

By delegating and elevating, you will build extensions of yourself that will enable you and your organization to continue to grow and develop. By not delegating activities to others, you will remain stuck.

Reflected one boss, "When I think of my own experience, I can see I've struggled to delegate things because I wasn't separating activities based on both my ability *and* desire to do them."

With that said, here is the painful truth. While this book will help you get past a lot of the personal head trash, you *must* get past it or you are destined to stagnate or find yourself replaced by a great boss.

Employees need to know that you trust them to do the work that you've delegated to them. Are you willing to let go of many of the activities that you've become good at doing but that are not the best use of your time?

Chris Beltowski of imageOne shared, "Applying the concept of delegating and elevating took me to a whole new level as a leader. It was an eye-opener that showed me how I could use my time better and grow as a leader. I was getting bogged down in everything and did not allow myself or my team to grow."

Great bosses appreciate that the return on investing time in their people is exponential to the results that it reaps. Leading and managing people is the number one role for a boss. You can't escape that fact. The more direct reports you have and the more diverse their roles, the more time a boss must devote to leading and managing. So look at the activities that you placed in the four quadrants and ask yourself, "Do I really have the emotional, intellectual, physical, and time capacity to be a great boss?"

Assuming that you've answered yes, you're ready to take another step towards becoming a great boss.

CHAPTER 4

surrounding yourself with great people

> *"The best executive is the one who has sense enough to pick good people to do what he wants done, and self-restraint enough to keep from meddling with them while they do it."*
>
> —THEODORE ROOSEVELT

ARE YOU SO CONSUMED BY YOUR WORK that you've missed your kid's birthdays, school activities, or ball games? While on vacation, do you continue to check in with the office, make business calls, check email, and worry about how things are going without you?

Have you ever felt like employees are wasting valuable time? They are there to distribute the workload and help you get more things accomplished—but you're not. In fact, you find yourself losing patience with the time it takes to get employees up to speed, so you continue to do some of their work. You rationalize that this is easier than training them or having to correct their mistakes. Then you discover that you're actually working longer hours but not getting any more work done. No small wonder that you're frustrated with employees that you hired to do the work but who just don't seem to listen or care.

As a boss, you have the opportunity and responsibility to choose the people that you want on your team. Even if you've been recently promoted or hired and have inherited several direct reports, remember that you must choose whether or not you want them on your team. Choosing your team is a privilege that bears great responsibility. Choose carefully and correctly.

Great bosses take time to evaluate their teams. In this chapter, we'll show you how to complete an assessment of your team to ensure that your people fit your culture, using the same standard that you apply to yourself: Do they get it, want it, and have the capacity to do it?

In a *New York Times* interview published on March 13, 2010, Kip Tindell, CEO of the Container Store, shared one of his foundation principles: "One great person could easily be as productive as three good people. One great is equal to three good. If you really believe that, a lot of things happen. We try to pay 50 to 100 percent above industry average. That's good for the employee, and that's good for the customer, but it's good for the company, too, because you get three times the productivity at only two times the labor cost."

Similarly, in *Good to Great*, Jim Collins shared the comments of one Nucor executive who said, "We have the hardest working steel workers in the world. We hire five, work them like ten, and pay them like eight."

Think about your organization. Are you certain that your people are working to their full potential? If you believe the Gallup Poll results we shared in chapter one, you probably have some people rowing harder to make up for those who aren't rowing at all. It's not fun, it's not fair, and it's not very profitable. And guess who leaves the boat first? Not the people who've been along for the ride. Most likely, it's the rowers. They have more options and will go where they're rewarded and recognized. And when they leave, the boat will slow down, take on water, and may even eventually sink.

The first step that you must take to surround yourself with Great People is to define what *you* mean by great. One organization's definition of Great People will not be the same as another's. Creating your definition of great is essential to building a cohesive, effective team. Here is a simple definition:

"Great People" are the Right People who are in the Right Seats.

It's a deceptively simple statement, but don't be fooled. Defining the Right People and getting them into the Right Seats requires some explanation, along with a couple of tools.

Many bosses miss the mark when hiring people. They copy what they read or hear about other company cultures and Great People in other companies without applying the criteria to their specific situation. You must clarify your own definition of what a role entails. You must also be willing to do the work that's necessary to define your culture, and then select people who fit your culture—who get it, want it, and have the capacity for the job. This is the first step needed to create an environment where people are actively engaged. The following is a powerfully simple way of helping you get all the Right People into the Right Seats.

DEFINING "RIGHT PEOPLE"

In *Built to Last*, Jim Collins discovered that enduring companies have a culture that defines who they are, what they value, and what attracts like-minded individuals to them. Your Core Values drive your culture. Core Values define the soul of an organization—what truly matters. They endure because they guide organizations through "moments of truth" when they're put to the test. People who fit the culture know what to do because they can feel why it's important. Conversely, those that don't fit the culture feel out of place.

Patrick Lencioni explains in his article, "Make Your Values Mean Something," for the July 2002 *Harvard Business Review*, that Core Values already exist. You can't make them up. They are discovered, meaning that they are already there, lying just below the surface. In the next few pages we will show you an exercise that will help you illuminate them.

Too often, the marketing department, human resources, or a committee of employees concocts Core Values and then illustrates them on posters, business cards, T-shirts, and websites. Unfortunately, most of what's heralded is fiction. The Core Values sound nice but few people in the organization believe them or live by them.

Core Values should always be "discovered" by the Leadership Team. When communicated to the entire organization, Core Values should come as no surprise to the people who share them (the Right People). On the other hand, Core Values make those who don't share them (the Wrong People) apprehensive because they don't really believe in them. That's precisely the benefit of a strong set of Core Values—they define a culture that attracts people who have similar values and repel those who don't.

Dick Gill of Gill Security, a company specializing in home security systems, shared a story that exemplifies the power of his company's three Core Values: "Continuous Improvement, Customer First, and Old-Fashioned Work Ethic." Dick said, "While on a service call to ensure that an existing system was monitored, our technician Mike suggested that at a minimal cost, the customer should purchase a hallway smoke detector, thereby increasing the level of safety in their home (continuous improvement). Two years later, Mercedes, an employee responsible for monitoring security systems, noticed that the system serviced by Mike was not working properly. Mercedes called the customer and after reviewing the situation sent a technician to troubleshoot (the customer is our priority).

"When our service technician, Jon, arrived at the customer's home, he discovered that the phone system was no longer communicating with the monitoring station. He suggested a wireless solution, which they agreed to install the next week, as it was too late in the day to have it programmed. At this point, Jon could have left but he didn't want to leave the customer unprotected over the weekend. So he stayed late on a Friday night, ensuring that the phone line was communicating correctly (we honor an old-fashioned work ethic).

"Less than 24 hours later, the customer's mother accidently left something on the stove while she and the rest of the family had gone to bed. In the middle of the night the smoke detector (installed by Mike) detected smoke and via the working phone line (that Jon had stayed late to fix) notified the monitoring station, which in turn dispatched firefighters who arrived in time to extinguish the fire with minimal damage to the home. On Monday morning a grateful customer called our office to thank us for the care that we had shown."

There's no question that Mercedes, Mike, and Jon were the Right People and shared the company's Core Values of Continuous Improvement, Customer First, and Old-Fashioned Work Ethic.

Think about the people who you work with and who work for you. The ones that continually frustrate you likely don't value what you do. This is probably why you don't trust or respect them. You can try to talk to them, but from our experience, we know that it's impossible to change anyone's Core Values. Either they have them or they don't.

We sincerely hope that your company has a clearly defined set of Core Values. If you are a midlevel manager or supervisor in a company without clearly defined Core Values, we suggest that you urge the owner and Leadership Team to establish them. They will serve as a compass, as they did for the employees at Gill Security, to guide behavior that you want and need to build a great organization.

Follow the simple exercise on the next page to guide you through the process of discovering your Core Values.

DISCOVERING YOUR CORE VALUES

If you are the owner or a member of the Leadership Team, and you haven't already done so, we strongly urge you to discover your Core Values. Use the simple four-step method below to do so:

1. Think about three people in your organization today that you admire and that you wish you could clone. You know who they are. They're the ones that you wish others would emulate. Write down their names.

   _____   _____   _____

2. Now, think about the qualities, attributes, and characteristics that make these people such a valuable asset. If you had 100 people like them you could dominate your industry. Think about what makes them who they are—the things that you can't teach, that are inherent.

3. Write all these characteristics on a sheet of paper. When you've finished your list, carefully examine what you've written. Your Core Values lie somewhere within these characteristics. Choose the best three to seven (less is more) that clearly articulate exactly what you value.

   _____

   _____

   _____

   _____

   _____

4. Next, write each of them as short and sweet statements or phrases that require very little elaboration or definition. Often the right word or phrase resonates quickly with the "Right People" and is more memorable. As an example, one of our clients uses the word "foxhole" to express a Core Value of digging in and working well together. Another client uses "funergetic" to express a Core Value of having fun and bringing positive energy to work.

   _____   _____   _____

   _____   _____   _____

Here is an example of five Core Values from a real-world company:

1. Help First
2. Grow or Die
3. Be Humbly Confident
4. Do the Right Thing
5. Do What You Say

THE PEOPLE ANALYZER™

Once you clearly define your three to seven Core Values, you can determine if someone is a Right Person for your organization by using a simple tool called The People Analyzer. In the following example, we'll use the preceding list of Core Values to show you how the tool works.

Name	Help First	Grow or Die	Be Humbly Confident	Do the Right Thing	Do What You Say	
Herb						
Rita						
Curt						
Diane						

THE PEOPLE ANALYZER™

Diagram 4

Begin by listing the people on your team down the left-hand column and your Core Values across the top row. Next, rate each person based on how well they live (or don't live) by each Core Value. Base your ratings on personal observations of their behavior. In addition, take into account feedback from your peers. For each Core Value, you will give each person one of three ratings—a plus, a plus/minus, or a minus. This is the definition for each:

- A Plus (+) means that they live the Core Value "most of the time." No one is perfect.

- A Plus/Minus (+/−) means that "sometimes they do and sometimes they don't" live the Core Value—they're hot and cold.

- A Minus (−) means that "most of the time" they do not live that Core Value.

To create a useful assessment, you must be completely honest with yourself when evaluating your people. Trust your gut. In this process, you're creating awareness and exposing issues. After you evaluate everyone using The People Analyzer, you'll have a clear picture of who is living the Core Values, as in Diagram 5:

| THE PEOPLE ANALYZER™ | | | | | | |
Name	Help First	Grow or Die	Be Humbly Confident	Do the Right Thing	Do What You Say	
Herb	+/−	+	+	+	+	
Rita	+/−	+/−	−	−	+	
Curt	−	−	+	+/−	+/−	
Diane	+	+	+	+	+	

Diagram 5

We will come back to this tool in a couple of pages to set a minimum standard and create absolute clarity around what defines the Right People for your organization. First, let's see what we mean by the Right Seat.

DEFINING "RIGHT SEAT"

A "seat" is a function that reports to you as the boss. What makes it a seat is that you have defined exactly what you expect of the person who is going to fill it. Each seat has about five Major Roles and Responsibilities that summarize at a high level the accountability or job description for that seat.

To define a seat, list its five Major Roles and Responsibilities. Keep them simple, not a laundry list of activities; in this case, less is more. This will clarify expectations for the person sitting in that seat.

Next, you must give the seat a name (Title). Again, a seat is simply a function, with its name and its five Major Roles and Responsibilities defined. Diagram 6 shows an example of a seat for an accounting function and its five Major Roles and Responsibilities:

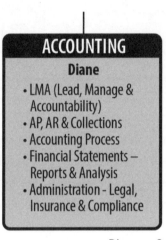

ACCOUNTING
Diane
- LMA (Lead, Manage & Accountability)
- AP, AR & Collections
- Accounting Process
- Financial Statements – Reports & Analysis
- Administration - Legal, Insurance & Compliance

Diagram 6

Next, determine all of the seats reporting to you that are critical to your department's or organization's functionality and growth—not necessarily what it looks like today, but rather what it must look like over the next six to twelve months to meet your goals. The objective here is to create absolute clarity for each direct report about where they should focus their activities and what their most important responsibilities are. Also consider adding any activities that you need to delegate to free up time for yourself.

With all of your seats defined, you are now ready to assess whether or not all of your people are in the Right

Seat. Again, do they get it, want it, and have the capacity to do that job (GWC™ for short)? Answer either yes or no for "G, W, and C." There are no maybes. Now go back to The People Analyzer, add GWC to the top row next to Core Values, and fill in your answers as in Diagram 7:

Name	Help First	Grow or Die	Be Humbly Confident	Do the Right Thing	Do What You Say	Get it	Want it	Capacity to Do It	
Herb	+/−	+	+	+	+	Y	Y	N	
Rita	+/−	+/−	−	−	+	Y	Y	Y	
Curt	−	−	+	+/−	+/−	Y	N	Y	
Diane	+	+	+	+	+	Y	Y	Y	

THE PEOPLE ANALYZER™

Diagram 7

When you are clear about your Core Values and the definition of a Seat, you can utilize The People Analyzer to determine if you have the Right People in the Right Seats. However, before you go any further, it is time to set the *minimum acceptable standard* in your organization. We call this "The Bar."

THE BAR

To complete The People Analyzer, you must first establish The Bar. This becomes your minimum acceptable standard for the Right People (aligned with your Core Values) and

Right Seat (GWC). As an example, we recommend that a company with five Core Values set The Bar at any combination of three plus ratings, two plus/minus ratings, and no minus ratings. The Bar for GWC ratings must be all yeses. And, each yes must be an emphatic YES. See the following example in Diagram 8:

Name	Help First	Grow or Die	Be Humbly Confident	Do the Right Thing	Do What You Say	Get it	Want it	Capacity to Do It	
Herb	+/-	+	+	+	+	Y	Y	N	
Rita	+/-	+/-	-	-	+	Y	Y	Y	
Curt	-	-	+	+/-	+/-	Y	N	Y	
Diane	+	+	+	+	+	Y	Y	Y	
The Bar	+	+	+	+/-	+/-	Y	Y	Y	

THE PEOPLE ANALYZER™

Diagram 8

If The Bar for Core Values is any *combination* of three plus ratings and two plus/minus ratings, and The Bar for the GWC™ is all yeses, anyone at or above The Bar is the Right Person in the Right Seat. As you can see in Diagram 8, Diane hits all of those benchmarks and meets your minimum acceptable standard for Great People.

Everyone else in Diagram 8 is below The Bar. Herb is the Right Person, but he's in the Wrong Seat because he doesn't have the capacity to do it. Rita is in the Right Seat, but she is the Wrong Person because she doesn't fully exhibit the Core Values. Curt is the Wrong Person and he's in the Wrong Seat because he doesn't really want it or fully exhibit the Core Values.

To summarize, Great People are the Right People in the Right Seat:

- The Right People are at or above The Bar of Core Values.
- The Right Seat means they have three yeses for G, W, and C.
- The People Analyzer is the tool used to assess both the Right People and the Right Seat.
- The Bar within your People Analyzer defines your minimum acceptable standard for Great People.

After completing The People Analyzer and establishing The Bar, you'll be prepared for the Four People Issues that you will have to deal with as a boss:

1. Right Person, Right Seat
2. Right Person, Wrong Seat
3. Wrong Person, Right Seat
4. Wrong Person, Wrong Seat

We'll be discussing the Four People Issues and how to deal with them in chapter nine. But in the meantime, you may be wondering why we consider a Right Person who's in the Right Seat an issue. To answer that, ask yourself a simple question: Of the Four People Issues, which one is occupying most of your time and attention? If you're like many bosses, you are spending most of your time with Wrong Seat issues like the Herbs and Curts. Meanwhile, the Wrong People (the Ritas) are undermining everything you're trying to do. Sadly, because you have to focus so much attention on these hires, the Right People in the Right Seats (Great People such as Diane) get very little of your time. That's an issue. In fact, that's a big problem. You don't want your Dianes leaving you for a more encouraging boss.

As Kelly Cuellar, director of operations for Zoup!, a restaurant franchisor, explains, "I learned long ago that to focus on the non-performing employees takes valuable time away from your great employees, and creates animosity. And what I learned recently is that your Great People may not come to you with issues and opportunities because they feel you are too busy, and they don't want to bother you. I have found that scheduling thirty to sixty minutes every month (sometimes more often) with each of my team members helps them feel I value their input, and that they are as important as any other aspect of the job. They have the floor, and they have my attention."

Imagine for a minute what your world could be like when you're surrounded by the Right People who are in the Right Seats. You must realize that this is possible and doable. We see it every day. Said one boss of a retailing company, "The difference between winning and not winning is a fine line. I made just one people change on our Leadership Team that created a very positive domino effect that transformed the company. In hindsight, I should have acted much faster! My hesitancy and discomfort around addressing a 'right person/wrong seat' issue created a six-month delay in performance that could have been avoided."

The People Analyzer now gives you a clear definition of Great People. Plus, it will help you improve your ability to select the Right Person for the Right Seat. The People Analyzer, along with The Bar, is an incredibly simple and practical tool used by tens of thousands of bosses all over the world. With this clarity you can now consistently hire, fire, review, reward, and recognize your people.

One of our clients, Dennis Burke of Sequoia Automatic, a manufacturer of air conditioning components for the automobile industry, enthusiastically embraced The People Analyzer as the most effective method for hiring, developing, and especially promoting people at his company. He said, "In the past we put people into seats based on 'Way Better Than' the person we replaced. That's how we created a lot of people issues for ourselves. We now use The Bar to ensure that we have Great People at every position within our organization."

You may also have put people into seats when you felt under pressure to fill empty seats quickly. This is all too common in many organizations. One of our clients referred to this hiring practice as "Better Than Nothing." We hope you agree that GWC is a much better standard for placing someone in the Right Seat.

As you go forward and build a strong team, we urge you to be relentless and inflexible when it comes to The Bar. Let it be the absolute minimum standard when it comes to defining Great People. Never accept mediocrity. Remember, Great People are your only competitive advantage!

When choosing a candidate to join your team, their People Analyzer assessment at a minimum must look like Diagram 9. To be above The Bar, they must possess any combination of three plus and two plus/minus ratings for Core Values along with three yeses for GWC.

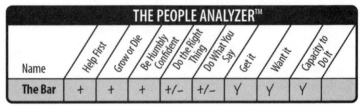

Diagram 9

To paraphrase Teddy Roosevelt, are you a boss who has sense enough to pick good people (who share your values and get it, want it, and have the capacity) to do what you want done, and self-restraint enough (as in letting go and delegating) to keep from meddling with them while they do it?

With the groundwork laid in these first four chapters, the stage is now set to get to the heart of what makes great bosses. By definition, great bosses lead, manage, and hold their people accountable. In the next chapter, we will show you the most effective way to do all three.

CHAPTER 5

leadership, management and accountability (LMA)

"We struggle with the complexities and we ignore the simplicities."

—Norman Vincent Peale

IN CHAPTERS ONE THROUGH FOUR we laid a foundation for the next three chapters, which are the crux of this entire book. We urge you to keep returning to these three chapters from time to time because they serve as a compass to keep you on course toward becoming a great boss.

This chapter sets up a baseline for everything that comes next. Let's look at the big picture first. What really will separate you from the pack? We'll start with a guiding principle: *A great boss creates a work environment where people are fully engaged and highly accountable.*

How would you rate the level of accountability in your organization on a scale of 1–10 (where 10 is high)? If you're like most of the bosses we've interviewed, you rated accountability low, usually a 4. It's one of the many "people issues" that frustrate bosses. You assign jobs to your people, only to be frustrated when they don't follow through and accomplish them.

Before we get to the heart of what you must do to become a great boss, there are Four Truths that you must embrace, because if you don't, none of what you read here will matter.

THE FOUR TRUTHS

Truth 1: Being a Great Boss Can Be Simple

Thousands of books have been written on leadership and management. They can be confusing, contradictory, and tie you up in knots with theory and complexity. Some will list thirty or more characteristics that you must have and dozens of things that you must do. This is an example of what Norman Vincent Peale is describing when he states, "We struggle with the complexities and we ignore the simplicities." The truth is, if you do five things consistently as a leader and five things consistently as a manager, you will be a great boss. It's that simple!

Truth 2: Your Style Does Not Have to Change

It doesn't matter if you're nice or tough, introverted or extroverted, charismatic or reserved. Just be yourself. When you are authentic, you are more believable and you will build trust. Don't be intimidated by what you read regarding high-profile leaders who have lots of charm, or worry that you'll never measure up to their larger-than-life personalities. You don't have to change your style. You have to be you for people to believe in you.

Truth 3: You Must Genuinely Care About Your People

You can't fake it. Your people will know if you care about them. There's an old saying: people don't care what you know until they know that you care. You could still apply what we will teach you in this chapter and you'll be pretty good. However, if you don't care, you'll never be great. It's like trying to be a great parent but not really caring about your kids.

Truth 4: You Must Want to Be Great

There's no middle ground here. You must genuinely desire to become a great boss. That means being willing to invest the time necessary to continuously improve yourself. For your business to grow, you must grow. If you don't want to put in the effort, none of what we teach you will stick. After all, the title of this book is *How to Be a* Great *Boss*.

Assuming that you embrace the Four Truths, let's get to work.

As a boss, you must fully provide your direct reports with effective leadership and management. This takes time. Sometimes you've failed to provide both because you've become overwhelmed by the 136 things that you're involved in and you don't have the time to lead and manage your people. If this is the situation you find yourself in, go back to chapter four and apply the learning from the Delegate and Elevate exercise to free up and devote the right amount of time to your people. When you don't have the time to lead and manage, accountability slips, because it comes from being a great leader *and* a great manager. You can't demand accountability or wish for it. You must create it by applying a simple equation:

Leadership + Management = Accountability (L+M=A)

There is a distinct difference between leadership and management. Leadership involves working "on" the business. It entails providing clear direction, creating an opening for people, and taking time to think. Management, on the other hand, involves working "in" the business: creating clear expectations, communicating well, and ensuring that things get done. Diagram 10 illustrates these points:

LEADERSHIP	MANAGEMENT
• Working "on" the Business	• Working "in" the Business
• Clear Direction	• Clear Expectations
• Creating the Opening	• Communication
• Thinking	• Doing

Diagram 10

Being a great leader doesn't make you a great manager and vice versa. To become a great boss, you must consistently do five things as a leader and five things as a manager. We call these things "practices" because it takes consistent *practice* of each of the five to become great.

Here is another way to describe the difference between leadership and management: Vision and Traction. Leadership consists of creating a Vision, and Management consists of gaining Traction to achieve it. You cannot succeed without both.

One of the most prolific inventors of all time clearly understood this. Thomas Edison, among other notables, said, "Vision without execution is hallucination." We tell our clients a variation of the same thing: "Vision without *Traction* is Hallucination." A lack of either or both frustrates everyone. In fact, "lack of growth" is another one of the most common frustrations that bosses share with us. Great bosses (those who lead and manage) understand the importance of having a Vision *and* the Traction necessary to achieve it. Growth is the outcome of having both, as Diagram 11 illustrates:

VISION - LEADERSHIP	VISION WITHOUT TRACTION Hallucination	VISION WITH TRACTION **Growth**
	NO VISION OR TRACTION Nightmare	TRACTION WITHOUT VISION Rudderless

TRACTION - MANAGEMENT

Diagram 11

As we are about to do a deep dive into the practices that make for great leaders and managers, we need you to think about all the people that report directly to you. Depending on the size of your organization or department, they typically number one to eight, possibly more if you supervise people who perform essentially the same type of work. Regardless of the number, we need you to hold that number in your mind. As we take you through the Five Leadership Practices™ in chapter six, and the Five Management Practices™ in chapter seven, we'll ask you for an all-or-nothing response. We will state the practice, teach the practice, and then ask you to answer yes or no as to whether or not you are doing the practice. For you to answer yes to each practice, you must be doing it with *all* of your direct reports. If you're failing to do one of them with one or more of your people, you must answer no.

Be completely honest with yourself. You're creating awareness of the gaps you must bridge, the skills you must apply, and the time you must invest to truly become great. So, don't kid yourself. Let's start with the Five Leadership Practices.

CHAPTER 6

the five leadership practices™

"The essence of leadership is to get others to do something because they think you want it done and because they think it is worthwhile doing."
—DWIGHT D. EISENHOWER

U.S. PRESIDENT AND FIVE-STAR GENERAL Dwight D. Eisenhower used a simple exercise to illustrate the art of leadership. He laid an ordinary piece of string on a table and explained, "Pull the string and it will follow you wherever you go. Push it and it will go nowhere at all. It's just that way when it comes to leading people."

PRACTICE 1. GIVING CLEAR DIRECTION

Great leaders are masterful at providing a clear direction and creating an opening for their people. When you create an opening, it produces a vacuum that is always filled.

As an example, our number one goal at EOS Worldwide is to help ten thousand companies implement EOS, Entrepreneurial Operating System®. This goal both provides direction and creates an opening that focuses and motivates everyone in our organization to rise up, move toward it, and achieve it.

When President John F. Kennedy proclaimed on May 25, 1961, that we would put a man on the moon and return him safely to Earth by the end of the decade, he in effect created an opening for the team at NASA to seize the opportunity, make it happen, and launch us into the Space Age.

An example more closely related to your position is the thinking you need to do about hiring people. In chapter four, we provided you with an example of a seat necessary for your organization to grow. As you define additional seats for your organization, think of each one as an opening, an opportunity for people at or above The Bar to rise up and fill those seats.

The best way for you to create an opening and provide clear direction for your people is by sharing a compelling vision. This consists of conveying clarity around your culture, your core focus, and your goals. You lay out where you're going and how you'll get there.

Creating a compelling vision is a collaborative effort by a company's Leadership Team to answer the following eight key questions:

1. What are the **Core Values** that define who you are—your company culture? (see the exercise we shared with you in chapter four)

2. What is your **Core Focus™** that articulates why you exist and what you do best?

3. What is the **10-Year Target** that creates the opening to inspire and motivate your organization?

4. What is your **Marketing Strategy** that defines your ideal customer and the message that attracts them to you?

5. What is the **3-Year Picture™** that creates an image of what your organization will look like in the not-too-distant future?

6. What is your **1-Year Plan** that clearly establishes your financial objectives and three to seven goals for the year?

7. What are the **Quarterly Rocks**—the three to seven most important priorities that must get done in the next ninety days to ensure that your yearly goals will be met?

8. What are the **Issues**—the list of ideas, opportunities, obstacles, and barriers to address and resolve both long term and short term?

For a comprehensive how-to manual on answering The 8 Questions™ read *Traction: Get a Grip on Your Business* by Gino Wickman. By answering these eight questions with absolute clarity, you will have a comprehensive vision to share with your people. This will ultimately create an opening and provide your people with clear direction. If you are in a midlevel management position and your company's Leadership Team has already done this work, then simply share this vision with your people. If your Leadership Team hasn't completed this work, urge them to do it.

After you've shared the vision with your people the first time, we urge you to continue to share it with your team every ninety days. Your people will need to hear it repeated at least seven times for it to sink in fully. A tried and proven method to do this is through the Quarterly State-of-the-Company Meeting. It works as shown in Diagram 12:

QUARTERLY STATE OF THE COMPANY MEETING

This meeting has proven to be the most effective discipline for helping people share, understand, and buy into the company vision. In its purest form, the meeting has a three-part agenda:

1. Where you've been;
2. Where you are;
3. Where you are going.

Each quarter, the leadership team fills each of those agenda items with three of the most relevant data points, and delivers a clear, concise, and powerful message that keeps people in the know. Its effectiveness stems from delivering it every quarter and being consistent.

Diagram 12

There is a huge difference between shared *with* all and shared *by* all. The former means that you've started the process, while the latter means that you've finished the process.

This is where many organizations fall short. They assume that by sending a company-wide email or newsletter, everyone will share the vision. We stress the importance of sharing the vision every ninety days at a minimum.

A boss in an employee-benefits company shared this: "We created a 'shared by all' game plan, starting with Quarterly State-of-the-Company meetings where we shared our performance, communicated our goals, and recognized people who exemplified our Core Values. Department heads then cascaded the message down through their teams. The enthusiasm was contagious and helped to accelerate our success."

Knowing that giving clear direction means conveying a compelling vision often and creating an opening, you should ask yourself, "Do I provide clear direction for every one of my direct reports?" Please honestly answer yes or no.

PRACTICE 2. PROVIDING THE NECESSARY TOOLS

Once you've provided clear direction for your people, you must give them the tools and support they need to succeed. Necessary tools include such resources as training, technology, additional people, and your personal time and attention.

Of all resources that you can provide, the most important one is your personal time and attention. Ironically, this resource is the least expensive to provide, but when you don't have the few hours per week that one of your people may need, the cost in terms of poor communication, stalled projects, and lower productivity can be enormous.

Kris Marshall of Winning Futures shares this experience: "I recently hired a business development person whom I carefully trained to use our sales process and marketing materials. After working with this person closely, I felt confident in his ability to represent our organization and effectively sell our services. However, weeks later I observed that he was losing his enthusiasm and just not having fun. After having a one-on-one-conversation, I realized that I had failed him. Despite the training, I hadn't given him the time he needed to thoroughly understand why and how we do the things we do a certain way. So, we started going out on sales calls together, where he could observe me in action and I could observe him. It didn't take long to get him refocused and reenergized. We still do check-ins and I occasionally accompany him on calls. I make the time to spend with him on a regular basis, and it has made a world of difference."

Another boss shared this story: "I was responsible for employees and clients all over the country. Whenever I traveled to see my clients, I seldom met with my employees in that city. I was always in a hurry to get back to my office and missed the opportunity to spend time with them. As much as I had preached about the importance of making time for our people, I certainly wasn't walking the talk."

When your people need your time and you don't have it, you must free yourself up, using the Delegate and Elevate tool discussed in chapter three, or you will fail them.

While your time is vital for your people as a resource, don't lose sight of other vital resources such as training, technology, and additional people. The way to find out if they have all the necessary tools is simply to ask them. It's debilitating to get your people excited about the direction you're headed, only to fail them by not providing the necessary tools to get the job done. It's like giving a blueprint to a contractor to build a house but then withholding the necessary tools or materials.

In Gallup's Q12 Survey™, employees were asked the question, "Do you have the material and equipment you need to do your work right?" Many answered "no." The experts at Gallup noted that this lack was highly emotional for many employees; often the needs may be very basic.

So, think about what you want your people to build. Then ask yourself, "Am I providing the necessary tools (including my time and attention) for every one of my direct reports to succeed?" Yes or no?

PRACTICE 3. LETTING GO OF THE VINE

Now that you've provided clear direction and given your team the necessary tools to succeed, it's time to let them run with it and get the heck out of their way. Unfortunately, this is easier said than done. Many leaders either can't or won't let go.

There's a story to illustrate this. A leader is walking along the edge of a cliff. Suddenly, he slips and falls over the edge. As he's falling down the side of the cliff, he manages to grab onto a vine. He finds himself hanging on for dear life, hundreds of feet from the top of the cliff and hundreds of feet from the bottom. In desperation, he considers a prayer to the heavens, and shouts, "Is there anybody up there?"

To his utter amazement and relief, a deep voice booms down from the clouds and asks him, "Do you believe?"

He's desperate, and with nothing to lose, he yells back, "Yes!!! I believe!!!"

The voice replies, "Then let go of the vine."

Terrified, the leader hesitates and gasps, "Is there anyone else up there?"

Now, before you just let go, we must share an important disclaimer: *you cannot let go until you are certain that you have the Right People in the Right Seats.* You must have direct reports to whom you can let go—reports who get it, want it, and have the capacity to do it (GWC). When they do, they'll be able to rise up and seize the opportunity you've given them. If they don't, you *cannot* let go of the vine. Until you fill these seats with the Right People, whoever is currently in the seats will always pull you into doing all or some of their work. You'll never have the time you need to be an effective leader or get things done.

So, you cannot take this third Leadership Practice and haphazardly let go, or use it as an excuse. You can't say, "Well, they told me to let go, so I did and I failed." It is incumbent on you to ensure that each direct report has the Core Values, gets it, wants it, and has the capacity to do it *before* you let go.

Daniel H. Pink, author of *Drive: The Surprising Truth About What Motivates Us*, points to three major factors that directly influence a person's level of motivation: Autonomy, Mastery, and Purpose. In this Leadership Practice, we are focusing on the first motivation, *Autonomy.* Your people want the freedom to do what you've hired them to do, and they can get frustrated when you meddle with them while they're trying to do it. Give them some rope, the freedom to succeed, to show you what they can do. You become a better leader when you clarify the outcome you are looking for and then let your people achieve that outcome in their own way. Even though it might not be the way *you'd* do it, you'll still get the right outcome.

A boss shared his observation about the benefit of letting go and how doing that helped his team: "My first reaction to the concept of 'letting go of the vine' was to look at my people and think of the countless situations where they had failed to make decisions to help us reach our long-term goals. I had serious doubts about their ability to make key decisions independent of me.

"However, my top-down leadership approach was not helping them grow. As an example, our typical meetings were high-tension affairs that produced mediocre results. My team would offer up information and I would make all the decisions. It wasn't until I missed one of our critical meetings that I realized my error. In my absence, there was great collaboration without any tension. However, no decisions were made.

"I was upset that they had not made progress while I was away. Then it hit me! Despite telling my team that they were in charge, I realized that I was the one who was actually doing their work. I was the one holding on to the vine, holding them back and not trusting the people in the company to make decisions. I did, in fact, have Great People that wanted to fulfill our vision, but I just hadn't allowed them to do it.

"It was time for me to let go of the vine and let them carry the company toward our vision. I realized that my team was already aligned with the direction of the company, and they were committed to helping it grow. They needed someone to lead them, not someone to tell them what to do. The more I let go, the more they grew and the faster we achieved our goals."

In a session with one client, a boss complained that he didn't have enough time to get his job done because he had people lined up all day outside his office. He commented that perhaps he should purchase a pull-tab device similar to what you use at the butcher shop so people could "take a number." He thought he was being funny, but he was talking about a very serious failing. He was taking pride in having all the answers for his people. He was hanging on and controlling everything. By not letting go, he was robbing himself of the time he so badly wanted for other duties. It was making him feel powerful, being the go-to guy, but he was not empowering his people to answer their own questions. As a result, he was creating his own problem.

In his book, *The One Minute Manager Meets the Monkey*, Ken Blanchard reminds us: "Don't take on the problem if the problem isn't yours. That monkey doesn't belong to you." A "monkey" could be a problem, obstacle, barrier, or anything that your direct reports bring for you to address and solve. All too often, the boss feels she must take on the monkey, the question or issue. Here's how it works. All day your direct reports knock on your door asking for advice, or for you to make a decision for them or to give them a quick answer. Picture that question or issue as a monkey on their shoulder. They're bringing that monkey to you. And their number one goal is to leave you with their monkey.

What do you do? More than likely, you've been taking their monkeys. This process goes on all day. By the end of the day, you have twenty monkeys all over your office to deal with, leaving you frustrated, exasperated, and overwhelmed. Don't take their monkeys. You're not addressing the underlying problem. You need to create autonomy, but instead you're enabling people to give you their problems to solve.

The solution is for you to make sure your people walk out of your office with their monkey. It's okay to serve as a sounding board, but limit your involvement to that. A great way to cure this epidemic is when they bring a monkey to you, ask them to bring a solution or two. Ask them, "What would you do?" Regardless of the technique you use, just ensure that when they leave your office, they take their monkey with them.

So, here's the question: "Am I letting go of the vine with every one of my direct reports?" Yes or no?

PRACTICE 4. ACTING WITH THE GREATER GOOD IN MIND

Ask yourself, "Am I walking the talk? Am I setting the example?" This means that whatever vision you've conveyed to your people, your actions and decisions are aligned with that message. The irony is that once you put the needs of the company before your own, you'll get everything you want and more. As Warren Bennis said, "A leader doesn't just get the message across, a leader is the message."

In his book, *American Icon: Alan Mulally and the Fight to Save Ford Motor Company*, author Bryce G. Hoffman shares a key point in the turnaround of Ford that Mulally led. He writes, "Ford executives finally stopped making decisions based on what was best for their own careers and started trying to figure out what was best for the company as a whole." Hoffman goes on to say, "It was the key to Ford's phenomenal resurgence." Acting with the greater good in mind resulted in one of the greatest turnarounds in American business history, led by one of the greatest leaders of our time.

The compelling vision that you conveyed to your people in Leadership Practice 1 is the greater good that we are describing here. Once you have done this, all of your actions must align with that greater good. All the words in the world mean nothing to your people if you don't back them up with your actions. "Do what I say, not as I do" doesn't work. Remember, your people are watching you, and before they commit to change, they will evaluate how well you walk the talk. *As go you, so go they.* You must consistently act with the greater good in mind.

To ensure that his people always act with the greater good in mind, Todd Sachse of Sachse Construction has a discipline he has used for decades. He calls it "The 10, 10, 10 Rule." He explains that the first 10 represents the *first ten minutes* after making a decision. Emotion usually drives your initial reaction. How do you feel about the idea? Are you happy, sad? The second 10 represents the *first ten months* regarding a decision, which he considers short term. You usually ask yourself, how much money am I going to make this year? What resources do I need and what will they cost me? The third 10 represents the *first ten years* after a decision. Now you're asking yourself, how will it affect my reputation, relationships, community, and family?

Todd urges you always to evaluate the third 10 as the most important in all decisions. When you make decisions based on the long-term greater good, you begin each decision-making process by thinking about how the decision will affect relationships, the company's reputation, and the future.

Coincidentally, Suzy Welch teaches the exact same discipline in her book *10-10-10: A Life-Transforming Idea*, which reinforces the importance of always acting with the greater good in mind.

Todd teaches this discipline to all of his people to help them focus on the greater good. To illustrate the importance of this approach when making decisions, Todd's company landed a high-profile, $18 million project. Halfway into the project, however, he realized they were going to lose $750,000, due to multiple mistakes by many parties.

Upon this realization, Todd concluded that blaming, finger pointing, and lawsuits would just exacerbate an already bad situation. What he cared about was his company's reputation. He made the decision to focus on the greater good and emphasized this point with his team. He told them, "We are not going to focus on the money. We are going to do the right thing and make it perfect and move on, because our relationships and reputation are more important in the long run." Todd understood that no amount of money could repair a poor reputation.

The troops rallied and erected a showpiece that indeed became the talk of the town. Despite the short-term profit loss, the project gained them considerably more work and profit over the long run. This is a classic example of acting with the greater good in mind.

How well are you living up to this practice? Ask yourself the question that Winning Futures founder Sam Cupp would ask: "Do you want to do what's best for the company, or do you want to do what you want to do?" Sam's business grew to more than twenty-five companies totaling $300 million in revenue. He always acted with the greater good in mind, making him both a successful businessman and a great boss.

Here's a confession from a boss who wasn't so great at acting with the greater good in mind. She started working for a small company, where she had to wear many hats and be involved in many departments. As the company grew, she reached her capacity and needed to delegate and elevate, but she resisted because her sense of worth came from having control over multiple functions. When her boss eventually hired a new person to take over two of her functions to free up her capacity, she was resentful. She also felt that she was less valued and wallowed in self-pity. Six months later, she finally realized how much happier and focused she was in her new role. Upon reflection, she appreciated that the change has been for the greater good of the company, a change that she did not appreciate at the time because she had let her ego get in the way.

So, now is the moment of truth. Ask yourself, "Do my actions, decisions, and personal example align with the company's greater good?" Yes or no?

PRACTICE 5. TAKING CLARITY BREAKS™

To stay sharp, confident, and at your best for your people, you must take Clarity Breaks.

One discipline that all great leaders have in common is that they take time on a regular basis to rise above the everyday demands of their jobs to reflect and think from the thirty-thousand-foot level. As Henry Ford said, "Thinking is the hardest work there is which is probably the reason so few engage in it."

In his book *The 7 Habits of Highly Effective People*, Stephen R. Covey calls this discipline "sharpening the saw." Bill Gates calls it "think weeks." He would take one week twice a year to do just that—think. Lee Iacocca wrote in his autobiography about how, when he was running Chrysler, he would take time each Sunday night to establish his goals and prepare for the upcoming week. He started this practice while in college. All great leaders have their own formula. Therefore, you must choose yours. Decide the time, place, and frequency that works best for you—whether it's daily, weekly, or monthly.

By definition, a Clarity Break is time that you schedule away from the office, out of the daily grind of running the department, to think and to work *on* your business, department, or self. Stepping back to think will create clarity for you and restore your confidence. This is important because the normal course of day-to-day business pulls you deeper and deeper into the minutiae of your work. As a result, you sometimes can't see the forest for the trees. You start to feel overwhelmed and you become short with your people.

Therefore, at intervals, you must elevate yourself above the day-to-day activities "in" the business so you can work "on" the business. As the philosopher Kurt Gödel stated: "You cannot be inside of a complex system and at the same time understand the system you are in." Choose a day, time, and place that works best for you. Some leaders think longer range in their den every morning, or at a library weekly, or a coffee shop monthly. Never do a Clarity Break at your office.

Schedule an appointment with yourself. Put it down on your calendar. If you don't schedule the time, it will never magically happen. At first you may be concerned about when you'll find the time. The irony is, you'll actually save time by taking Clarity Breaks. When you are clear about your bigger objectives, you gain the confidence to simplify procedures and create efficiencies. You make better decisions when you're not under stress.

Use this scheduled break wisely, though. This is not time to catch up on email or complete a to-do list. It's time to think, to see things clearly and restore your confidence. Faced with a blank legal pad or journal, with no agenda, no interruptions or distractions, you'll be challenged at first to actually *think*. After all, you're starting to form a new habit. Henry Ford was right—it is the hardest thing to do. To help you get started, we've listed some questions you can ask yourself during a Clarity Break:

- Is the Vision and Plan for the business/department on track?
- What is the number one goal?
- Am I focusing on the most important things?

- Do I have the Right People in the Right Seats to grow?
- What is the one "people move" that I must make this quarter?
- How strong is my bench?
- If I lose a key player, do I have someone ready to fill the seat?
- Are my processes working well?
- What seems overly complicated that must be simplified?
- Do I understand what my direct reports truly love to do and are great at doing?
- Am I leveraging their strengths?
- What can I delegate to others in order to use my time more effectively?
- What can we do to be more proactive versus being reactive?
- What can I do to improve communication?
- What's my top priority this week? This month?

In the October 15, 2015, issue of *Financial Advisor*, Deena Katz related an experience that she had while on a cruise ship in the North Atlantic. She found herself completely disconnected from the outside world when her ship lost its internet connection for five days. Without any electronics to keep her occupied, she found herself sitting around with nothing but time. As she wrote: "In final desperation, with absolutely nothing else to do, I began to think. I thought about my clients, our next generation of advisors, some processes that we needed to refine and some marketing strategies. I let the ideas flow, then began to take notes. What resulted were solutions to an array of items that had needed attention for a long time, but that I really never thought I had time to attack. There was no interruption, no input but thoughts I generated. I was synthesizing and analyzing the morass of data I had collected in my head for decades. This is the essence of critical thinking."

Chris Beltowski of imageOne shared this about how taking time to think helped him: "At one point I was stressed while wearing too many hats and overseeing far too many people. I took a Clarity Break and was able to see clearly the way my world looked at that moment in time and what I thought it should look like for the greater good of the company and my own sanity. I formulated a game plan, shared it with the owners of the company and was surprised at how quickly they gave me the okay to move forward. Forcing myself to take that Clarity Break helped me to see things from a completely different level."

Our clients regularly tell us of similar experiences. After taking their very first Clarity Break and seeing the benefit, they eventually began to schedule them regularly. So, ask yourself, "Am I taking Clarity Breaks?" Yes or no?

THE LEADERSHIP SELF-ASSESSMENT

Now that you have a clear understanding of the Five Leadership Practices, we've created a one-page self-assessment so you can do a quick checkup on yourself. Answer each statement either yes or no. Remember, it's an all-or-nothing answer.

LEADERSHIP SELF-ASSESSMENT		
	Yes	**No**
1. I am giving clear direction		
• Creating the opening		
• A compelling vision		
• Eight questions		
2. I am providing the necessary tools		
• Resources		
• Training		
• Technology		
• People		
• Time and attention		
3. I am letting go of the vine		
• Delegate and Elevate™		
• Right Person in the Right Seat		
• Not meddling, getting out of their way		
4. I am acting with the greater good in mind		
• Company Vision		
• My actions		
• My decisions		
• Walking the talk		
• Company needs first		
5. I am taking Clarity Breaks™		
• Focusing "on" the business		
• Creating clarity		
• Protecting my confidence		
• Scheduling them daily, weekly, or monthly		
• Using a journal or blank legal pad		

Diagram 13

THE FIVE LEADERSHIP PRACTICES—NEXT STEPS

Step 1

If you've answered the self-assessment questions honestly, you probably have one or more no's. This exercise is not trying to make you feel guilty or inadequate. Rather, it is intended to show you the areas that need improvement so you can become a great boss. So put a stake in the ground. Schedule a date on your calendar for when you will be able to answer yes to all of your no's. The norm is six months from today.

If you answered no to any of the questions in the Five Leadership Practices and you don't know how to change that no to a yes, go back to that practice. Reread that section and apply exactly what we taught.

Step 2

Schedule a date, time, and place on your calendar to take your next Clarity Break. Right now.

How do you become a great leader? Remember what President Eisenhower said: "The essence of leadership is to get others to do something because they think you want it done and because they think it is worthwhile doing." By giving clear direction, providing the necessary tools, letting go of the vine, acting with the greater good in mind, and taking Clarity Breaks, you will become a great leader. This is one-half of the formula to become a great boss!

Now that you know how to be a great leader, let's address how to become a great manager.

CHAPTER 7

the five management practices™

"Effective leadership is putting first things first.
Effective management is discipline, carrying it out."
—Stephen R. Covey

REMEMBER THE EQUATION. Being a great Leader plus a great Manager equals Accountability (L + M = A). Also, remember there is a distinct difference between the two.

To start this discussion on management, let's admit the truth: you can't "manage someone." Management is not what you do *to* someone; it's what you provide *for* someone. If you're feeling like you have to manipulate or overly manage someone, you have a people issue. As Jim Collins states in his book *Good to Great*, "The moment you feel like you have to manage someone, you've made a hiring mistake." Management boils down to five basic practices. To the degree you do them well, "accountability" will be the byproduct. You'll get everything you want out of your people without their feeling "managed."

PRACTICE 1. KEEPING EXPECTATIONS CLEAR

A boss will often ask us, "How do I hold my people accountable?" The answer is that without clear expectations, you can't. Therefore, you must begin by setting clear expectations. Great managers communicate to their direct reports in crystal-clear terms what role they are to play. Yet this practice does not work only from the top down. Just as your direct reports must understand your expectations of them, you must understand their expectations of you. It's a two-way street.

If you're honest with yourself, you probably aren't being that clear about your expectations of your people. Here are the four areas in which you must have clear expectations:

1. **Roles.** Let's return to the five major roles, responsibilities, and accountabilities for the Right Seat that we covered in chapter three. You owe it to each of your people to clearly

articulate at a high level the work and outcomes for which they're being held accountable. Our recommendation is to boil it down to five major roles. If necessary, you can provide specifics with a detailed job description. But start at a high level.

2. **Core Values.** As we shared in chapter four, these are the inherent qualities that ultimately define your culture and the soul of your organization. You must teach your people the company's Core Values so they know exactly how you expect them to act and make good decisions in your absence that align with the organization's culture.

3. **Rocks.** These are quarterly key priorities (often referred to as goals, objectives, or initiatives). We prefer to call them "Rocks," a term made popular by Stephen R. Covey and Verne Harnish. It is vital that you and your direct reports agree on the one to seven most important priorities that they must complete in the next ninety days. When your direct reports are completing Rocks that are specific, measurable, attainable, realistic, and timely (SMART), they are more engaged in moving your organization forward. To be clear, set them *with* your people, not *for* your people. Here's how:

ROCK SETTING PROCESS

Step 1.   Share your company's annual Goals and quarterly priorities (Rocks)

Step 2.   Create your team's Issues List—topics that include obstacles, barriers, problems, ideas, etc.

Step 3.   With the company's Goals, Rocks and your team's Issues List as context, ask your direct reports, "What do you see as the most important things that must get done in the next ninety days?"

Step 4.   Make them SMART (specific, measurable, attainable, realistic & timely)

Step 5.   At the end of the rock setting process each of your direct reports should be clear on their Rocks for the Quarter

Diagram 14

4. **Measurables.** These are also known as metrics or key performance indicators. When each person has one or more numbers to measure their performance, it gives them a clear picture of whether or not they're winning. When each of your people has numbers to hit, it is the essence of pure accountability and clear expectations. There is nothing clearer than a number. Numbers give you data, the facts. And, as John Adams stated so eloquently, "Facts are stubborn things." When we expect people to achieve a certain level of productivity, supervising them becomes much easier because the measurement adds a level of objectivity. We're able to cut through assumptions, egos, opinions, and emotions—and focus on deliverables.

While creating a scorecard for his transportation company, P.B. Industries, Andrew Park challenged his team to think carefully about which numbers could predict success or failure. The head of safety felt that "accidents" (a trailing indicator) would be a good number to track weekly. Andrew asked him what activities would be good predictors (leading indicators) of when an accident might occur. The head of safety cited three poor behaviors by drivers: failure to take their legally required thirty-minute breaks, hard braking, and speeding. Onboard units were monitoring each of these things, so they became the measurables that Andy reviewed weekly with his direct reports. This brought tremendous focus to safety in general and helped identify drivers who were clearly below The Bar.

Given the concept of "measuring," you might feel a little uncomfortable or believe that your people might feel uncomfortable being measured. Please know that collaboration and competition are not mutually exclusive. We didn't survive as a species without competing for food and collaborating together to find it, kill it, and eat it. They're both ingrained deeply in our DNA. That's why knowing whether we're winning or losing keeps us focused.

Think about any sporting event that you enjoy either as a participant or as a spectator. What keeps you focused? It's *measurement*. It's the numbers! In golf, the leader board summarizes each individual golfer's scorecard and tells you where every player stands versus par for the course. In football, hockey, and basketball, it's the scoreboard. Imagine for a moment watching your favorite sport without a scoreboard. How engaged would you be? How engaged would the players be? You want to know whether your team is winning or losing—and by how much. That's what keeps everyone fully engaged. You measure the game by those results.

Let's apply this to business. How can we expect to get the most from our people if we don't provide them with a number or numbers that they are held accountable for delivering each week? There is an often-heard quote, "Employees respect what management inspects." Without a number, people expend energy on staying (or appearing to be) busy instead of focusing their energy on activities that truly generate results. Great bosses appreciate effort, but they focus on results.

Anna Saville of JA Frate, shared this story about the value of everyone having a number: "Years ago, as a member of the Operations Team for a local trash hauler, we were challenged to increase driver productivity. With input from the drivers and information about their coverage area, we set daily targets with them for *average pick-up time*, *number of containers*, and the *number of stops* that they could complete. With these measurements in place, we were able to challenge the drivers to increase their productivity. We posted their results daily, and at the end of each week, the drivers that made their goals had their name placed in a hat for a drawing for a $500 fuel card. We were able to watch the productivity numbers skyrocket as the stops per day increased and the time at each stop decreased."

Numbers don't lie. As with facts, they also are stubborn things. You delivered the numbers or you didn't.

If you're struggling to identify measurables to establish with your direct reports, here's a short list of examples from many industries to get your gears turning:

- Sales appointments scheduled
- Proposals submitted
- New deals closed
- Errors made
- Customer complaints
- Defective parts
- Product returns
- A/R greater than forty-five days
- Service times
- Utilization rate
- Customer satisfaction rating
- Overtime hours
- Billable hours
- Ancillary sales

Now that we have you thinking about measurables that may apply to your department, let's get back to our earlier point. Expectations are a combination of all four areas: Roles, Core Values, Rocks, and Measurables. When you keep your expectations clear, you will rarely have to fire anyone that does not meet them. They will usually quit because they realize they can't live up to your expectations. This is the healthiest and fairest approach.

Paul Ruby, general manager of the Herrington Inn in Geneva, Illinois, keeps his expectations clear through "The Herrington Rules—Creating Guests for Life," which he emphasizes with all employees. We've summarized them here:

1. Let guests know what you can do, not what you can't do.

2. Turn a problem into an opportunity to create a guest for life.

3. Believe that to serve others is to serve oneself.

4. Never allow guests to do something for themselves that you can do for them.

5. Make each guest feel special, as if they were our only guest.

6. The guest is not always right, but what matters is that they are still our guest and need to stay that way.

7. Be consistent—remember that you're "on stage" all of the time.

8. 15–10–5: Focus your attention on any guest within 15 feet; smile and make eye contact with any guest within 10 feet; and greet any guest within 5 feet—never turn your back to a guest.

9. Anticipate, follow up, and be proactive.

10. Assume that anyone who walks in the door is a VIP and treat them as such.

11. Take responsibility and use your best judgment.

12. Do it right the first time. Make a positive first impression.

Similarly, Eric Ersher of Zoup! has "14 Zoupisms" for the employees at every one of his 150 franchises to make sure they are clear on the Zoup! expectations and that the company maintains consistency in every location no matter where it is in the country.

Now let's go back to the idea that setting clear expectations is a two-way street. Once you've made your expectations clear to your direct reports, you must now ensure that you understand their expectations of you. You can accomplish this by asking, "Now that I've shared my expectations of you, what do you expect of me that will help you win?" You need to take their response to this question very seriously and deliver on their expectations. Otherwise, you can't expect them to deliver on yours.

As an example, your direct reports may request certain technology (hardware or software), they may need more of your time than they are currently receiving, or they may need to hire a person to get the job done. It's important that you hear them out and are honest regarding what you can provide them to succeed. That's precisely why this is a two-way street.

Once you know what your direct reports expect of you and they know your expectations of them, you can answer yes to this first management-practice question: "Am I keeping expectations clear with every one of my direct reports?" Yes or no?

PRACTICE 2. COMMUNICATING WELL

Now that expectations are clear, communication is vital. This is also a two-way street. Regard it as an opportunity to make sure you're in sync. Unfortunately, bosses often assume they're in sync with their direct reports because their people don't openly challenge or disagree with them. They also assume that their direct reports are dissatisfied or upset, when in fact they've simply misread them.

A great litmus test to prove you are communicating well is that you know what is on each other's mind. There are no assumptions in the relationship. Don't ever assume that people are upset or mad at you. Ask! Too many managers are just afraid to ask. They see the odd look on someone's face and they fail to ask, "What's up?" They make assumptions rather than trying to understand what that odd look truly means. When you think about it, most of the conversations you hear around the office concern assumptions that people make of each other. Don't assume. Ask! Here are four methods that have helped bosses eliminate assumptions and greatly improve their communication:

1. Two Emotions

A discipline that will help you avoid making assumptions about how someone is feeling and instead better understand them is called "two emotions." Here's how it works. When you're unsure what someone is thinking, ask, "If you could share two emotions about how you are feeling right now, one positive and one negative, what would they be? You share your two emotions and I'll share mine." This is an excellent way to open a dialogue and find out exactly what's going on with them. You are encouraging them to share their range of emotion from the highest to the lowest so that you have a clear perspective of how they are feeling.

For instance, while presenting your marketing plan, you notice one of your direct reports taking a deep breath, folding his arms, and frowning. You *assume* that he's not on board and might undermine your hard work. You decide to engage him by asking him to share two emotions. Here's how: "Frank, I had a tough time reading you during the meeting this morning, and I would love to know how you are feeling about it. What is the most positive and the most negative emotion that would describe how you're feeling about what you heard me say? You share yours and I'll share mine." Listen carefully to Frank's reply. He might surprise you by saying, "I'm excited about the possibilities but very concerned about whether or not we'll have the resources needed to make it happen. I didn't hear you talk about how we're going to pull it off." You now realize that your assumption was wrong.

After listening to your direct report, it's now time for you to share your two emotions. The power of each of you sharing one positive emotion and one negative emotion is that it helps you understand the range of how you both feel. And because this conversation requires both of you to be completely open and honest, it will help you build a stronger relationship.

2. Question-to-Statement Ratio

A great communication discipline is to monitor your question-to-statement ratio when having a conversation with your direct reports. If you're like most managers, you do most of the talking. Frankly, this one-way-street behavior needs to change. Your job is to ensure that the dialogue is 80/20, where your direct report is doing 80 percent of the talking and you're doing 20 percent. The only way to make that happen is to ask questions instead of making statements.

Ask "why, who, what, where, and when" questions. The typical manager, when presented with a problem, makes statements such as, "You should have done this . . ." or "Don't do that . . ." You'll be amazed what happens when an issue is brought to you, and instead of making a "You should have . . ." statement, you ask the person a question along the lines of, "Knowing what you know now, what would you do differently next time? Or, "What would you do?" Get them to answer the question. They'll become more independent. The more they talk, the more they will convince themselves they can handle their own issues. You'll have fewer monkeys to deal with and you'll get more things done.

For instance, imagine yourself as a boss dealing with someone who is repeatedly late for work. It's negatively affecting your entire department because other people have to fill in for him by taking incoming calls. When you meet with him, begin the dialogue by asking him what is causing him to be late. He tells you that there are mornings when he, not his spouse, is responsible for getting their kids off to school. You ask him what he *would* be able to do to get his kids off early enough for him to get to work on time. By asking him what he *would* do, you are in effect asking him to commit to his own plan for being on time.

Think about it. Who has the monkey? That's right—he does. He's taking responsibility and holding himself accountable. Asking him to solve his problem is more effective than repeatedly telling him to be on time.

One great boss who mastered this communication method had it validated when her direct report said out of the blue, "I just want to say thank you for never dictating or telling me what to do."

3. Echoing

Another discipline to help you become a great communicator is "echoing." Here's how it works. When you're in a situation where you told your direct report something and you're not entirely certain that they understood you, ask the following question: "Just to make sure that I am communicating well, could you please tell me what I just told you?" Or, if you're not sure you understood something they just told you, ask, "Here's what I just heard you say. Did I hear you correctly?" Don't be surprised or depressed by the response, because most of the time the message is not clearly received the first time. It then becomes a great opportunity for both of you to restate your message until you've eliminated any miscommunication and have gotten yourselves in sync.

4. "Thump-Thump"

One of our clients calls miscommunication between two people "thump-thump." He coined this term after he shared a study conducted by Stanford University psychology graduate student Elizabeth Newton, in which pairs of students faced each other. One student had a list of well-known songs such as "Row, Row, Row Your Boat," "Happy Birthday," "Twinkle, Twinkle, Little Star," and so on. That student would tap out a song on the table while the other student tried to guess the song. Of 120 songs tapped out, the listeners guessed only 3 correctly, a success rate of just 2.5 percent. The lesson here is that when a person is tapping a song on a table, they hear the song perfectly in their head, but that's not what the listener is hearing. They are hearing monotone thumps on a table.

When we share a verbal message with direct reports, the same thing often happens. We assume that we're doing a great job communicating—it's pitch-perfect in our heads. But the reality is that the other person is hearing monotone thumps—hence, "thump-thump." So next time, don't assume the message was clearly received. Ask, "Could you tell me what you heard me say?" You'll be a more effective communicator.

The objective when using any of these four methods is to become a great communicator and avoid making assumptions. After reflecting on each one, you may realize that you are already using one or more of them. Use them all and you will definitely make your communication more effective.

With the four methods clear, it is time for your answer: Are you communicating well with every one of your direct reports? Yes or no?

PRACTICE 3. MAINTAINING THE RIGHT MEETING PULSE™

You can leverage effective communication by instituting a rock-solid Meeting Pulse. We recommend that you have a consistent meeting cadence. Pull your team of direct reports together every week for sixty to ninety minutes. What gives weekly meetings a great pulse is that they are on the same day every week, start at the same time, have the same agenda, and they begin and end on time. Ensure that there is an even exchange of dialogue in these meetings. Each person should report measurables and results. In the process, you should identify, discuss, and solve the issues. For the perfect agenda, go to **www.eosworldwide.com/level-10** to watch a short video on how to run an effective meeting.

Look at the three examples of circles in Diagram 15 and picture them as the possible relationships between you and a direct report. Your job as a manager is always to keep your circles connected. The weekly Meeting Pulse is a great way to do that.

Example 1   **Example 2**   **Example 3**

Diagram 15

The first example illustrates what it looks like when you don't spend any time with your direct report. You're disconnected. In this scenario, it's inevitable that something bad will happen. Not because either of you are bad or deceitful. You're just not on the same wavelength about the company's objective or each other's expectations.

The second example is also ineffective. This shows you smothering them. They are under your thumb. You are micromanaging and not letting go. You are not letting them run with an assignment. Someday, especially if they're good at what they do, they will get frustrated and leave. Conversely, if they aren't good at what they do, you will be destined to carry their load forever.

The third example, where you've established just the right touch points, is the ideal. You are "keeping the circles connected," spending enough time with each other at regular intervals. You have this dynamic when you have a weekly Meeting Pulse.

It surprises us, when prescribing a weekly Meeting Pulse for teams, when a boss reacts negatively. She says, "I don't have time for a weekly meeting." That's like a salesperson saying "I don't have time for selling." A weekly meeting with your team is how you stay in steady contact with your team. We could share hundreds of stories where a boss resisted at first, finally caved, started holding weekly meetings, and loved them. They ultimately realized that communicating on a consistent basis saved them time and helped them get more things done.

Here's a sample from the hundreds of excuses that we hear from bosses before they finally commit to a weekly Meeting Pulse:

- I don't have time for meetings.

- Meetings are a waste of time.

- Meetings are boring.

- We don't have that many issues every week.

- It's impossible to get everyone together for a meeting every week.

- I have an open-door policy, so we talk all the time.

- If they need to talk to me, they know where they can find me.

- I meet with my people when necessary.

Now let's turn to what we hear from those same bosses just a few weeks later, after they begin a weekly Meeting Pulse with their direct reports:

- We're communicating better.

- We're coming together as a team, being more open.

- We are finally solving issues that have lingered for months.

- We're better at doing what we say we will do.

- In total, I'm actually spending less time in meetings.

- We're getting more things done.

- We're beginning to hold each other accountable.

- Everyone is being heard.

- I have a better feel for what's happening and why.
- We're having more fun.
- The team is more energized.
- My direct reports have a better understanding of our overall goals.

If you are resisting a weekly Meeting Pulse, we urge you to try it for ninety days and see for yourself.

The experience, expertise, performance, and behavior of each of your direct reports may vary greatly. For most, the weekly Meeting Pulse should keep them on track. However, some direct reports may also require one-on-ones, especially if they are new to your organization or their function. Some require that you meet with them once a month; others, each week. Determine the appropriate Meeting Pulse to ensure that each person receives enough of your time and that your circles stay connected.

One boss said this regarding weekly one-on-ones: "I really like them. I like the opportunity to touch base with each of my people one on one each week. I want them to feel in the loop, give them my ear, and let them know they have my attention."

At first you might consider one-on-one meetings to be micromanaging or think holding them weekly is over the top. Before you judge, decide on a case-by-case basis what works best for you and your people to keep the circles connected. For the boss we just quoted, holding a weekly one-on-one with everybody worked. As we pointed out in chapter five, your style doesn't have to change. This boss's style was more hands-on. It's very possible that you may decide you prefer these weekly one-on-ones, too, but most bosses we know don't do them. Instead, they use a weekly Meeting Pulse with their entire team of direct reports.

However, you may need a more frequent Meeting Pulse with someone who is newly hired or is new to your department. Think about all the things going through the mind of a new member of your team in their first ninety days. What do they think about all day? Think about their questions. Put yourself in their shoes. By ramping them up fast and investing more time up front, you will actually save time in the long run. The old adage is so true: "What starts well, ends well."

Giving your time and attention to new employees during their first ninety days will quickly pay dividends. You will discover whether they truly exhibit your Core Values. You will learn whether they get it, want it, and have the capacity to do what you've hired them to do. This will give you the opportunity to address any issues quickly, nipping them in the bud before they become bigger. And you will get them up to speed faster.

So, ask yourself, "Do I have the right Meeting Pulse, and are the circles connected with every one of my direct reports?" Yes or no?

PRACTICE 4. HAVING "QUARTERLY CONVERSATIONS"

To truly manage and continue to improve your relationship with each of your direct reports, you need to connect at a higher level in addition to the weekly Meeting Pulse.

To accomplish this, you must have a face-to-face Quarterly Conversation™ with each direct report. This is an informal conversation to talk about what's working and what's not. It's *not* a performance review, and it's different from a one-on-one meeting, where you're focusing on immediate issues. This conversation should be held off site, over coffee or lunch, but never at your desk—that's too formal. It's also important to hold the Quarterly Conversation where you won't be interrupted, where you can speak openly, and where you'll be free from distractions.

The Quarterly Conversation should focus around what we call "The 5-5-5™," as illustrated by Diagram 16:

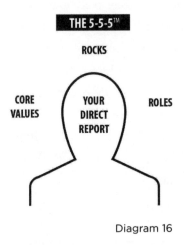

Diagram 16

This diagram serves as a visual reminder, when you are looking at your direct report, to keep the conversation focused on why you are together. Ninety percent of what you expect of your people falls into the categories of Core Values, Rocks, or Roles. The objective is to discuss what's working and what's not working in these three areas. By openly discussing these opportunities for improvement in the Quarterly Conversation, you will be able to make wonderful little course corrections in your relationship, which as a result will keep getting better and better. We call it the 5-5-5 because there are usually three to seven Core Values, one to seven Rocks, and four to six Roles (the average for each is about five). And it's easier to remember the numbers "5-5-5" than "6-3-4."

Conduct the conversation on a quarterly basis because, in our experience, relationships begin to fray and goals tend to get off track about every ninety days. It's human nature: at the beginning of the period you're both feeling 100 percent clear about your objectives and the plans that you've made. Then life happens.

Consider this: A few weeks after you are both 100 percent on the same page, you find yourself unexpectedly assigned to a task force. Then your wife signs you up to be a Little League umpire, and your dog gets sick. Meanwhile, your direct report reads a business book and starts experimenting with what he's read. Then he gets pulled into multiple issues in his department. His wife volunteers him to coach his kid's soccer team. His cat has kittens. Five months go by before both of you finally come up for air. You realize that your objectives and well-crafted plans are way off track. With all that has happened, how could you possibly remember what you agreed to five months ago? That's the fray we're talking about.

As the boss, you must take the first step to keep the relationship from fraying. You have to catch it just before the fray begins, usually around the ninetieth day—hence, a *Quarterly* Conversation.

Another reason to meet every quarter is that time flies by and, before you realize it, after six months of solving tough issues you may learn that you no longer have a strong and healthy relationship with your direct report. Here's what one boss had to say about catching the fray just before it begins: "I had given an Annual Review to a team member, and before I knew it, the entire year had gone by and it was time for another review. Although we were meeting weekly to review projects, we weren't really talking about the expectations that I had communicated in the Annual Review and, as I discovered, our relationship was a little strained—my expectations were not as clear as they once were, nor were they being met."

Due to the importance of this practice, we will do a much deeper dive in chapter eight to help you master it. We have a complete set of practical suggestions to help you make your Quarterly Conversations with each of your direct reports highly productive and constantly improving.

So ask yourself, "Am I having Quarterly Conversations with every one of my direct reports?" Yes or No?

PRACTICE 5.
REWARDING AND RECOGNIZING

Whether they give a pat on the back or a kick in the butt, great managers reward and recognize their people quickly. Napoleon Bonaparte observed, "A solider will fight long and hard for a bit of colored ribbon." Studies show that people work harder for recognition than they do for money. Although the money is important and you must pay your people fairly, acknowledgment counts for a lot. Don't underestimate the power of recognition and the effectiveness of feedback, both positive and negative. Here are three recognition disciplines that will help.

1. The 24-Hour Rule

Always give positive or negative feedback quickly, ideally within twenty-four hours. Waiting any longer than that to give positive feedback reduces its impact. It won't seem genuine and could be perceived as an afterthought. And waiting to give negative feedback until you have a laundry list is ineffective and puts people on the defensive. They'll shut down and often miss your message. It leads to resentment and failure to change behavior. So, giving feedback within a day will change the behavior that you want.

2. Public and Private Recognition

As you give positive and negative feedback, you should always criticize in private and praise in public. Never mix either of these up. Criticizing people in public will destroy whatever level of trust that you have built with them and damage your relationship. On the other hand, recognizing and celebrating someone's achievements in private misses the opportunity for someone to shine in front of their peers.

To expand a little on this topic, whenever you have constructive criticism for one of your direct reports, always give it in private, as most can handle it behind closed doors. And when you have praise, always give it within earshot of as many people as possible. A great idea is using companywide meetings as a platform to recognize people in front of their peers. This fills most people up. It's like fuel. You're energizing them to work harder for everybody around them.

3. Boss versus Buddy

It's also important to always be their boss, not their buddy. It's okay to have a friendly relationship with direct reports, but you must understand the fine line between being in charge and being in the trenches. Don't cross the line. If you do, you'll never be a great manager. When the line is blurred and you consider them more of a friend, you can never fully apply these practices due to potential hurt feelings, or having to tiptoe around tough issues and dilute the real message.

Here's a poignant story about what happened to a boss when she allowed the line between boss and buddy to become blurred: "One of my employees and I were good friends and we worked very well together. We had an agreement that in the office I would be the boss. It worked great for many years. On day-to-day supervision, performance evaluations, and constructive criticism our interactions worked smoothly. However, when the recession arrived and business declined, never-before layoffs were required. During this layoff process, I had to lay off my good friend. As a result, this employee never forgave me and we were estranged. I was heartbroken. Following that experience, I never became buddies with my employees. I only had great business relationships with them. However, after I retired, I began to socialize with some of them and we became good friends."

———————

If you have difficulty patting your people on the back, as many managers do, put a monthly reminder on your calendar to do so. This may sound terrible to have to be so calculated, but if that's not a natural instinct for you, make yourself remember. This practice has such a huge effect on your people. One great boss followed this monthly calendar discipline for two years until praise became a habit. Now he naturally gives recognition; it's become second nature to him.

Whether by reminder or habit, you may also be one of those people who are not good at coming up with ways to praise others. If this is your problem, try one of the following:

- Simply say, "You're doing a great job!"
- Or, "I really appreciate what you did."
- "Thanks for speaking up!"
- "I'm glad you're on our team."

- Give them a personally written thank-you note.

- Give them a gift card.

- After they've put in long hours to complete a difficult assignment, send their spouse a thank-you note with a dinner certificate.

If those prompts are not enough to get you started, or if you're looking for more ideas, check out a great book by Bob Nelson, PhD, titled *1501 Ways to Reward Employees*. There you will find hundreds more.

THE THREE-STRIKE RULE

Sometimes, however, despite your best efforts to create clear expectations, communicate effectively, have Quarterly Conversations, and provide positive or negative feedback quickly, things don't work out. Your direct report fails to deliver and doesn't see or admit they are not delivering. Here's how to handle performance issues when you're thinking of firing somebody. It's called the Three-Strike Rule:

Strike One: Meet with the person, identify the issue(s), and agree on the course correction that must be made. The People Analyzer from chapter four is a great tool to show them a black-and-white picture of the issue, clarify your expectations, and determine how best to solve the issue. Put this feedback in writing to eliminate any misunderstanding. If you think it's necessary, have a third party sit in and witness the conversation. Give the employee one month to resolve the issue and set a time to meet again.

Strike Two: Meet with the person again and review the prior thirty days' performance. If the performance was at or above The Bar in The People Analyzer, the employee is meeting your expectations. Things are back to normal and you've solved the issue. However, if they are not meeting expectations once again, identify any remaining issues and agree on the plan to address them. Put your feedback in writing and, if necessary, have a third party witness the conversation. Give them another thirty days and set a time to meet again.

Strike Three: If the issue isn't resolved by the third meeting, terminate them. As a practical matter, when you apply the Three-Strike Rule effectively, most will quit before the third-strike meeting. This is why you will rarely have to fire anyone. They will leave because they can't live up to expectations that you've made clear to them.

Important: You should have at least three data points (specific examples) for each issue that you raise during each meeting in the Three-Strike process. The person will typically dismiss the first data point as a coincidence, and they can talk their way out of the second data point, but by the third data point, they'll say, "You got me"—it's clear that the problem is not an isolated one. Make sure that the person acknowledges and agrees that they're below The Bar before determining an appropriate action plan.

Hopefully, we've convinced you how important giving positive and negative feedback is to being a great boss. If so, ask yourself, "Am I rewarding and recognizing every one of my direct reports—both a pat on the back and a kick in the butt?" Yes or no?

MANAGEMENT SELF-ASSESSMENT

Now that you have a clear understanding of the recommended Five Management Practices, we've created a one-page assessment so you can do a quick checkup on yourself. Thinking of the people that report directly to you, complete the self-assessment in Diagram 17. Answer each statement either yes or no. Remember, it's an all-or-nothing answer.

MANAGEMENT SELF-ASSESSMENT		
	Yes	**No**
1. I keep expectations clear • Mine and theirs • Roles, Core Values, Rocks and Measurables		
2. I communicate well • Me and them • We know what's on each other's minds; there are no assumptions • Question to statement ratio • No "thump, thump"		
3. I have the right Meeting Pulse • Even exchange of dialogue • Reporting measurables • Keeping the circles connected		
4. I have Quarterly Conversations • Completing the 5-5-5™ • Using the People Analyzer™ (Core Values and GWC™)		
5. I reward and recognize • Giving positive and negative feedback quickly • Criticizing in private and praising in public • Being their boss, not their buddy • Applying the Three Strike Rule when necessary		

Diagram 17

Next Steps for Management Practices Self-Assessment

1. If you've answered honestly, you probably have one or more no's. This exercise is not intended to make you feel guilty or inadequate, but to show you the areas that need improvement to become a great boss. Just as with the Five Leadership Practices, put a stake in the ground for when you will be great. Schedule a date on your calendar when you will be able to answer yes to all of the questions in Diagram 17. The norm is six months from today.

    If you answered no to any of the Five Management Practices and you are feeling stuck or unclear about how to transform your response to a yes, go back to that practice, reread it, and apply exactly what we taught.

2. Review this management self-assessment one on one with each direct report immediately. Ask them how you are doing with each of the five practices. This will help you hear the truth, lead to a great dialogue, and make you a better manager.

To summarize chapters six and seven, you are a great leader when you provide your people with clear direction, give them the necessary tools, let go of the vine, act with the greater good in mind, and take Clarity Breaks. You are a great manager when you keep expectations clear with your direct reports, communicate well, have the right Meeting Pulse, have Quarterly Conversations, and reward and recognize. The byproduct of being a great leader and a great manager are personal accountability and therefore a highly accountable organization that you, the great boss, created. Keep working until you can answer yes to both the Five Leadership Practices and the Five Management Practices, hopefully with the next six months.

When you reach the point that you can answer yes to all of the Five Leadership Practices and Five Management Practices, you will eliminate any chance of hallucination. That's because you have a crystal-clear vison that everyone shares and knows how to carry out with superior execution.

Please come back to chapters six and seven once or twice a year. This review will serve as a great refresher and tune-up. Make it part of your lifelong journey as a great boss.

CHAPTER 8

the quarterly
conversation

"Look eye! Always look eye!"
—MR. MIYAGI in *The Karate Kid*

RARELY DO WE HEAR BOSSES express complete
confidence in their ability to coach, provide feedback, and
have completely open discussions with their direct reports.
Some of them start off with good intentions, but they're
overcome by anxiety about where the conversation might
go and what to do if the meeting starts to go badly. In effect
they talk themselves out of having an honest conversation,
rationalizing that it's better to let sleeping dogs lie. They're
just plain afraid to look their people straight in the eye and
have a *real* conversation.

This is why, in this chapter, we are doing a deeper dive into the practice of Quarterly Conversations. To the degree that you master this practice, you will improve your relationship with your direct reports, and ensure you're continually on the same page.

When we ask our clients to begin scheduling Quarterly Conversations with their direct reports, we're met with some skepticism and resistance. Here's what we hear:

- "I talk to my people all the time."
- "I'm already meeting with my people every day."
- "I don't know when I'll find the time to meet."
- "I don't want them bringing me problems, I want solutions."
- "I've been talking, but they're not listening to me."
- "Every ninety days? Are you serious?"

You may be thinking along the same lines. For many of our clients, the Quarterly Conversation is an entirely new and foreign discipline. So it's not too surprising that, at first, having them feels strange, even awkward. If you've ever tried correcting your golf swing, you know what we mean. At first, the new way feels awkward, but with practice, you're soon appreciating how natural it's become and how it's improved your game. The key is accepting that you must let go of what hasn't been working and commit to mastering a new method of communication.

A boss in an insurance company said, "Quarterly Conversations have had a direct impact on employee commitment and engagement. We know that when employees don't understand their role, they become disengaged. The conversations keep them on the same page with their manager. As a result, they feel like they are part of a team and they know how to help the company win."

We've been asked lots of questions regarding Quarterly Conversations. Here are some concise statements that will address most of them:

- Schedule the conversations well in advance.
- The point is the substance (the face-to-face, open, and honest dialogue), not the gesture.
- It's okay to take notes—for yourself, not for the employee's file.
- It's not a performance review.
- Don't meet them in your office; go off site.
- Let the 5-5-5 be your guide, not your master. Be prepared, but keep it simple.
- It's okay to be nervous—the Quarterly Conversation is a new experience for your direct report, too.
- The conversation is mutually beneficial; you'll each walk away with constructive feedback that will make you both better.

You'll learn, as all of our other clients have learned, how vital this form of communication is. You're looking each other directly in the eye, with a common objective to make each other better. Think of the benefits that this will have on your direct report, your relationship, your department, your organization, and finally on your confidence, peace of mind, and time. This will put you squarely on the right path toward becoming a great boss.

A quarterly timeframe works best because, as we mentioned in chapter seven, an understanding of shared objectives begins to fray around the ninetieth day. The business climate changes, the industry shifts, and you're continually challenged to meet customer expectations. There's a lot happening and if you neglect checking in, the circles with your direct reports become disconnected.

Again, the Quarterly Conversation is an informal, face-to-face, one-on-one meeting to talk about what's working and what's not working. It is not a performance review and doesn't require filling out a form. Too often bosses let the form get in the way of having a meaningful, open, and honest conversation. Think of the form as an obstacle between you and your direct report.

Have the conversation where you won't be interrupted or distracted. We strongly recommend that you do them off site. Focus the conversation around the 5-5-5—Core Values, Roles, and Rocks. These three areas encompass 90 percent of your expectations. Some of our clients refer to this practice as "having 5-5-5s" because it utilizes the 5-5-5 tool and it reminds them to keep the tool in mind during their meeting.

By having a Quarterly Conversation, you're giving each direct report your time and attention. Remember, dialogue is a two-way street—an opportunity for both of you to re-clarify expectations, to communicate well, to keep the circles connected, and, if necessary, make course corrections. While the conversation requires no documentation, it's helpful to prepare and take notes before and during the meeting. To keep the playing field level, make sure that your direct report comes prepared with notes as well. Remember, you're taking notes in order to *be prepared* for the conversation, not to *document* the conversation. We can't emphasize this distinction enough. It's not a performance review, it's a conversation.

Schedule these meetings well in advance. Putting your Quarterly Conversation with your direct report on your calendar builds anticipation—a powerful dynamic that comes into play as each of you think, throughout the quarter, of topics to discuss. There's heightened awareness of behaviors, accomplishments, and results. Looking forward to a set date will also help both of you to come prepared.

Think about what this arrangement means to your direct reports. It tells them that you care, that they're important to you. Putting the meeting on a calendar every quarter lets your people know that you're anticipating a need to meet— that you're being proactive. This helps them take a proactive approach as well. They'll come prepared to share what they feel is working and not working.

Contrast this with an unscheduled Quarterly Conversation pulled together at the last minute. There will be no buildup, no awareness, and no preparation. Worse still is when your direct reports have to remind you to have them, or they never happen because you failed to schedule them. When you forget or fail to meet with them, you are actually making them feel more like you don't care about them.

When you schedule the meetings for the first time, put your direct reports at ease. The fact that you're having the meeting away from the office will probably raise all sorts of red flags with them. They may be asking themselves, "Why are we meeting? Why not in the office? Did I do something wrong? Am I being fired?"

They'll be nervous and you'll probably be nervous, too. Acknowledge this at the beginning. You could say something like, "To make sure that you and I are always on the same page and keeping expectations clear, I want to meet with you every three months. This is an opportunity for us to talk where we won't be interrupted or distracted."

Prepare for the meeting by thinking about the 5-5-5. Imagine yourself looking your direct report in the eye and discussing with them what's working and not working within the context of Core Values, Roles, and Rocks.

The primary purpose of the Quarterly Conversation is to discuss two questions that are sides of the same coin:

- What's working?
- What's not working?

Let's examine each question.

WHAT'S WORKING?

Begin by asking them what is working. Let them share their accomplishments, tasks, or procedures that they feel are going well within the organization and with you as their boss. You should listen and try to understand the following:

- What are they most proud of accomplishing during the last quarter?

- How did they accomplish this?
- What process or procedure worked well?
- What obstacles did they have to overcome?
- Who was most helpful to them?
- Do they feel they're working on things that really matter?
- Do they feel appreciated for the work they do?
- Did you provide them with tools they needed?
- Did you keep expectations clear?

After they've shared what is working, it's your turn to share what you feel is working. This is an opportunity to recognize and thank them for their accomplishments, behaviors, and progress. Be prepared with some specific examples. Making general comments such as, "You're doing great" or "I'm hearing good things about you" without having examples comes off as insincere.

Remember that people will work harder for recognition than for money. Even though compensation is important, don't underestimate the power of positive recognition. And don't confuse excellence with perfection. You can heap praise on someone and still expect improvement.

- Tell them how much you appreciate the projects they completed. Ask them how that experience has prepared them to take on a larger project.
- Acknowledge that they are hitting their stride in their current position.

- Let them know how their contributions helped the organization meet its priorities.

To emphasize the importance of recognizing performance and giving positive feedback, one great boss shared this story: "I had a manager that was doing really good work, but in her first ninety days I would only give her direct feedback if she needed to improve or if she made a mistake. I didn't pat her on the back or give her praise when she did well. I was moving so fast that in my head everything was good, so I didn't say anything. During our Quarterly Conversation, when I asked her how she thought she was doing, she said that she thought she was doing well but really couldn't tell since I didn't give her any feedback. Wow, I felt terrible! And from then on I was aware and I was able to give her exactly what she needed."

WHAT'S NOT WORKING?

When asking this question, take the opportunity to create a safe harbor for flushing out issues and getting to the root cause. Let your report speak freely. Don't interrupt them. If you begin to hear something that you don't like or disagree with, don't be defensive or overreact. Just listen. When they hesitate or seem to stop talking, don't fill the silence. Wait to see if they want to add anything else. Sometimes what emerges after the pause is what they really meant to say.

In her book, *Willful Blindness: Why We Ignore the Obvious at Our Peril*, Margaret Heffernan defines willful blindness as "something we could know and should know but don't know because it makes us feel better not to know." Experts who conducted research on this subject discovered that when employees are asked the question, "Are there issues at work that people are afraid to raise?" Eighty-five percent responded yes.

Some people hold back because they fear reprisal. They've usually seen firsthand what happens to people who push back, who question, who challenge the status quo. They don't wish to be viewed as disloyal, dissatisfied, or difficult to deal with. Who would want to go through that pain when you can keep your head down and play it safe?

People also don't raise issues because of apathy. They've become numb to issues that have been raised time and again with nothing ever changing. This is why you have to be attentive and resolve any raised issues. You have an opportunity, especially with people who are at or above The Bar, to stop treating symptoms. When you dig to uncover the root cause of an issue, you have a way to solve it. This will ultimately resolve the issue of apathy.

Keep in mind, the question you are asking is, "What's not working?" This creates a safe harbor to have the dialogue. You're not asking, "Who's to blame?" Consider this dialogue:

YOU: Mary, thanks for sharing what's not working. You mentioned a couple of things. Can we start with the one that matters most to you?

MARY: Sure. It would definitely be how we solve problems during our department meetings.

YOU: Can you give me a recent example?

MARY: Well, last week Steve was trying to make a point about a problem we're having in shipping. He was struggling a little bit to explain the issue. I have to admit I was getting a little exasperated myself, but none of us really gave Steve much of a chance. We were all feeling a bit uncomfortable until you jumped in and gave us a suggestion. It sounded really good at the time and since no one had a better idea, we ran with it.

YOU: And ...

(15 seconds of silence)

MARY: Well, I don't think your solution helped much. In fact, the more I think about, it only sounded good because it seemed so easy. We tried to fix a difficult problem with an easy answer when we really should have had more input from the team. As you probably know, the problem isn't really fixed.

YOU: Yeah, I know that. In fact, it sounds like part of the problem is me. I shouldn't have swooped in with a quick fix. I should stop doing that. I was selling you guys short. So, what do we do now?

MARY: I've done some digging and have some thoughts that I'd like to put on our agenda for this week's department meeting.

YOU: Did Steve help you do the digging?

MARY: Yes.

YOU: I'm glad to hear that. I'll make a concerted effort not to jump in with any quick fixes. Mary, thanks for bringing this up. I really appreciate it.

As Margaret Heffernan points out, people who have the courage to raise issues don't do so to be difficult, but rather because they genuinely care about the organization. They're often the most loyal. Think about your Great People, those at or above The Bar. They're likely to be the most willing to tell you "what's not working."

So, do not assume that when your request for feedback from direct reports meets with silence, that there are no issues. The Quarterly Conversation represents a huge opportunity to break down the barriers and get to the issues—the real ones. The sad fact is that silence, willful blindness, exists in every organization. There may be some in your company or department. Be prepared to listen carefully.

Don't tell them what's not working; ask them what's not working. Build trust and ask probing questions to get to the root cause. Seek to understand the issue. When you create a safe harbor for them to share their concerns, you'll focus the conversation on the root cause and solution that are needed, not on finding fault. Keep in mind that while your direct report may be afraid or unwilling to raise issues within a group setting, they might be more willing to share those issues with you face to face.

While they share what's not working, you should be listening and trying to understand the following:

- What process or procedure is broken?
- How well do they understand the root cause of the issue?
- Was the solution to the problem directly within their control?

- Did they have the responsibility, accountability, and autonomy to act?
- Did they plan well and fail to execute?
- Did you fail them in any way?
- Did you provide them with the necessary tools to succeed?

When they're finished sharing what's not working, don't respond with your solutions yet. Just list the issues. Because now it's your turn to share what you feel is not working. Be prepared and keep your comments focused on what's not working. Your job at this point is to articulate, in a bullet-point fashion with some explanation, the things you feel aren't working.

Once you have a list of items that aren't working (sometimes you'll have only one and sometimes you'll have ten), it's now time to go into "solution mode." That's when you decide what can and can't be solved. You'll come up with ways to solve the issues during the next quarter. Be prepared to help, but remember to keep the monkey from ending up on your back. You may have to take one or two items to solve yourself, and maybe some you'll work on together, but don't volunteer to take their monkey. Use the following to frame your questions:

- Given how things turned out, what could they have done differently?
- When did they realize that there was a problem?
- What action did they take?
- What is their plan to address it so the issue won't recur?

- What resources will they need?
- How do they think you can help?
- Should they take action first and then let you know what they did, or should they make a recommendation first so you can then decide together what action they should take?
- How will you both know that you corrected the issue?

At this point, if you are like many of the bosses we work with, you are thinking, "Holy cow! I'm going to get inundated with a ton of issues. Some I won't be able to solve, and I know that some of my direct reports are just plain whiners!" To put your mind at ease, you are correct. We know that is going to be the case. First of all, to be great, you must know about all the issues (real or not); second, to reduce your anxiety, put the issues into the following three categories:

1. Ones that can't be solved
2. Ones that *you* must solve
3. Ones that *they* must solve

Ones That Can't Be Solved

These types of issues typically frustrate most bosses because they are a case of whining, or they can't be solved to your direct report's satisfaction, which leads you to feel guilty or anxious. Most of the issues on the list during a Quarterly Conversation fall in this category. Here's what is critical for you to understand:

- They just need a response, answer, or
acknowledgment!

I know this is hard to believe, but as a great boss, you have to get good at saying something along the lines of, "I hear you and I know it's an issue that's driving you crazy. What I need you to understand is that the issue that you are describing exists for the following reasons [state the reasons] and it's not going to change. I just hope you can live with it even though I know you don't agree with it."

As a great boss, you are going to disappoint people from time to time and you must learn how to take some grief every now and then. Knowing that will make you stronger. The truth is, most of the time the Right People in the Right Seats will say, "I understand and can live with it. Thanks for listening." Sometimes they will stew for a while and you have to live with some discomfort for a week or so, but they usually come around and accept it. Again, all they need is an answer. Most not-so-good-bosses don't give an answer or they say they'll provide a solution, but they procrastinate—because the problem can't be solved—and therefore let the frustration build.

Sometimes there isn't a good answer. Consider this: Your company is using a CRM that it has invested tens of thousands of dollars and hours to implement. One of your new direct reports, an expert on databases, complains to you that it is difficult to use and that there are better systems available. You know that he is correct. You acknowledge the current system's shortcomings but also let him know that there's no chance of changing to a new system in the near future. You ask him to live with the current system and for his support.

Ones That *You* Must Solve

Unfortunately, you have to take on and solve these issues, either by working with other bosses in the organization or with the owner. First, agree on a timeframe for solving it (day, week, month, or year) and then agree on the exact plan of attack for solving it so that you effectively manage your direct report's expectations.

Imagine a situation where your direct report comes prepared for your Quarterly Conversation with specific examples about a process that is not working. You ask several questions and realize that, indeed, the process is broken. You ask her what she would do to solve the issue. She suggests changing a key step in the process that will require reprogramming software and additional training. She agrees to complete a detailed plan with a budget for your review. You set a timeframe for putting the plan into action that includes getting the support of your peers and approval of your boss. You've met her expectations by helping her solve a problem. You've also created an opening for her to call out other opportunities to improve the company.

Ones *They* Must Solve

Ideally, you want to push as many of these issues down to them, especially when they are truly their monkeys. But you should use the same approach as the problems you must solve. First, agree on the timeframe (day, week, month, or year) when the issue will be solved, and then agree on a plan of attack for how your direct report will solve it.

If you've done a good job addressing the three types of issues during your Quarterly Conversation by monitoring your question-to-statement ratio, you'll have finished your entire lunch while your direct report is still picking at theirs!

With practice in developing a cycle of Quarterly Conversations, you'll begin to recognize the true abilities and potential of your people. As a result, you'll be able to coach them to consistently do better work than they thought they could.

THE ANNUAL REVIEW VERSUS THE QUARTERLY CONVERSATION

We're frequently asked how Annual Reviews fit with Quarterly Conversations. The quick answer is that they should complement each other, not conflict with each other. Unlike the Quarterly Conversation, which requires no documentation, you should document the Annual Review, have it signed by both parties, and place it in the employee's file.

Our recommendation is that during the year, you complete three Quarterly Conversations and one Annual Review with your direct reports. We also recommend that you not discuss pay raises and other changes in compensation during the Annual Review. This keeps the conversation focused on performance, not explaining the rationale behind a wage increase or lack thereof. Keep the review form simple and do not let it get in the way of a meaningful discussion.

Here's an example of a simple Annual Review form that many of our clients use:

THE ONE-PAGE ANNUAL REVIEW

Date:

People Analyzer™ Assessment:

Help First	Grow or Die	Be Humbly Confident	Do the Right Thing	Do What You Say	Get it	Want it	Capacity to Do It

1. Strengths and key accomplishments:

2. Area(s) that needs improvement:

3. Plan to get things on track:

4. Comments:

Name: Signature:

Name: Signature:

Diagram 18

So, if you want a more productive Annual Review, start by having productive Quarterly Conversations.

Here's a question for you. Do you look forward to giving or receiving performance reviews? If you're like most bosses, the answer is No! Why is that?

Well, please excuse this admitted rant regarding the typical annual performance review. Let's look at how it works and why it is so unproductive. Most companies employ performance reviews to give feedback to subordinates on an annual basis, usually tied to a pay increase. The boss scrambles at the last minute (after repeated emails from HR to get the reviews completed and the forms turned in) to use a rating scale of 1 to 5, where 5 means "excellent" and 1 means "needs immediate improvement." Most bosses avoid rating anyone as a 5 because they'll be challenged by their boss or the HR department for being too easy. They avoid rating anyone a 1 because that might (1) lead to conflict and (2) require them to take corrective action, which usually involves a long paper trail of verbal and written warnings.

Even more counterproductive, most bosses believe (or are told by their bosses) that giving anyone an excellent rating implies that there is no room for improvement. They're confusing excellence with perfection. Imagine how disheartening this is for people most deserving of an excellent rating. When told that a rating of 5 is impossible, what are they supposed to do? Work harder? Not likely. What usually happens is because they feel unappreciated, they become resentful, disengaged, and motivated to look for another place to work where performance and skills are rewarded and recognized.

The traditional annual performance review was well intended. It was created because most managers would not give their direct reports any feedback. So, HR had to come up with a solution. We don't know why HR added wage increases, but we suspect their friends in the finance department had something to do with it.

Not surprisingly, very few of our clients have told us that they enjoy giving or receiving performance reviews. Instead of a direct, face-to-face conversation, they stumble over a form, tiptoe around a discussion about the pay increase, and completely miss the substance of any issues through open, honest dialogue. Some bosses laughingly admit that they're on their sixth revision of the performance review form and that none of those revisions have helped improve employee performance. Does this ring any bells with you?

We characterize the traditional annual performance review as nothing more than an elaborate "superstitious dance" by two reluctant partners who hate dancing. It's time to stop dancing around a process that is clearly broken. Why should you adhere to a practice that erodes the relationship between bosses and their direct reports?

Rant ended.

Some of our clients have done away with annual performance reviews in favor of completing Quarterly Conversations throughout the year, but we're not suggesting that you go that far. Instead, do away with any disingenuous rating scales. Use the one-page Annual Review in Diagram 18. That way you can have an open and honest Annual Review in conjunction with Quarterly Conversations. When you use this alternative, you'll find Annual Reviews easier and more fun to do. You'll have fewer surprises because you'll have had open and honest conversations three times already that year. In fact, when you have an effective Quarterly Conversation with each of your direct reports, you'll be looking forward to the Annual Review, not dreading it.

In summary, the power of the Quarterly Conversation lies in its ability to improve both your working relationship with your reports and your company's performance in general. Maybe the first one or two conversations will feel uncomfortable, like learning to dance, but after the third or fourth one, you will hit your stride and start to create an open exchange.

Please note, you should never wait for a Quarterly Conversation to address behaviors or performance that you feel hurts the organization or your relationship. Remember the 24-Hour Rule that we discussed in the management practice of rewarding and recognizing in chapter seven.

Having an honest face-to-face dialogue with your direct reports, and building a relationship with each other that is completely open, takes patience and persistence. Take a lesson from Mr. Miyagi, who exhorted Daniel in *The Karate Kid* to "Look eye, Daniel-san! Always look eye!" As frustrating as the first steps to mastering it can be, the rewards are worth the effort. Stay the course and reap the benefits.

CHAPTER 9

the four
people issues

"To see what is right and not to do it is want of courage."
—Confucius

EVEN IF YOU APPLY EVERYTHING that we've shared with you in the previous chapters, and despite your best efforts, you'll occasionally have a direct report that isn't behaving or performing at or above The Bar—your minimum acceptable standard for Great People. You may find yourself hoping upon hope that they'll turn things around. However, a problem doesn't fix itself. Here we will show you proactive and constructive ways to deal with people issues.

When we don't address people issues, there are consequences for us, our department, and our organization. They're already hurting you, and there's no way to hide them. Everybody knows. Out of your earshot, they're talking. You have to trust your gut and do what's right for the good of all. Too often we fail not because of our people, but through lack of courage to address people issues.

On the surface it would seem that there are hundreds of people-related issues, but as we described in chapter four, there are actually only four.

THE FOUR PEOPLE ISSUES

1. Right Person, Right Seat
2. Right Person, Wrong Seat
3. Wrong Person, Right Seat
4. Wrong Person, Wrong Seat

You will undoubtedly encounter each one (if you haven't already), so now we'll explain how to address each one of them.

Issue Number 1: Right Person, Right Seat

How is Right Person, Right Seat an issue? After all, it is your definition for a great person. However, it will become an issue if you aren't giving those individuals your time and attention. Think about how they feel. On the one hand, they are the ones rowing harder to compensate for others that aren't rowing. They're the ones most likely to raise issues that are hampering your department's performance. On the other hand, when you spend what precious time you have for your people focused solely on resolving "wrong seat" and "wrong people" issues, the Great People may feel that you're taking them for granted. Without your recognition, they won't contribute to their full potential.

One boss shared that early in his career, after being promoted to a middle management position, he would meet his father-in-law monthly for a "businessman's lunch"—an informal chat. One day his father-in-law asked him who he was spending most of his time with: his good managers or his poor managers. He told him, "My poor managers, of course. They need me the most, and my job is to help them get better."

"Well," his father-in-law replied, "I wouldn't want to work for you. I'd be one of your best managers, but I'd rarely see you. Why would I continue to work for you if you didn't spend the time to help me get better?"

Think of the upside when you spend time with Right People who are in the Right Seats. They're the folks that are actively engaged at work. They're the ones who energize you, challenge your thinking, and make you a better boss. They're also the ones best equipped to fill any vacuum and rise up to seize an opportunity—to take the ball and run with it. You must give them your time. And one great way to do this is through the Quarterly Conversation.

When asking, "What's working?" ask what you can do to make them more effective. Ask what they would do to make the company or department even better. A good question is, "If you were running the department [or company], what would you do differently?"

When asking, "What's not working?" ask them what process or procedure should change or could be simplified. A good question is, "Where are the breakdowns happening, why are they happening, and what would you do to correct them?"

Sometimes what's not working with them is that they have become complacent. It's a clear sign that you haven't kept the circles connected. One great boss, a client of ours, shared that, early in his career, his boss called him into his office and began a conversation with a simple question: "How do you think you're doing?"

He said that this question from his boss made him a bit nervous, because in his heart of hearts he had to admit that he had been coasting, confident in the fact that his performance was head and shoulders above that of his peers. However, he had underestimated the expectations that his boss had of him. He had a lot of respect for his boss; as tough as he was, he genuinely cared about his direct reports.

After our client answered that he thought he was doing really well, his boss looked him straight in the eye and told him how disappointed he was with his lackluster performance. (To be blunt, the boss's exact words were, "You've been a big f—ing disappointment.") He could say these words because they had built a very strong relationship. His boss made it clear that he had higher expectations of his hire than he had of himself, and ended the conversation by asking him if he was up to the task of improving his performance.

The choice was yes or no . . . in or out. Our client went on to say that that conversation changed his life. He stepped up, met expectations, and eventually became the company's president.

Don't be afraid to challenge people who are at or above The Bar. If you're afraid that they've grown complacent, look at yourself in the mirror and ask yourself, "Have I myself grown complacent? Have I accepted average performance or performance that isn't keeping pace with the demands of the business?" Challenge them to think outside the box, to take risks and act with the greater good in mind. And let them run with it.

Finally, thank them for their contributions. No one should feel that they are being taken for granted—especially those who are at or above The Bar. They're the ones that accept responsibility, admit when they fall short, and quietly deliver the results week after week. They need to hear that they're appreciated. They might not need compliments every day, but hear them they must. Keep the circles connected.

With the next three people issues, we will offer you a process for how to solve them. We urge you to check with your HR professional and labor attorney to ensure that they are in alignment with your company policies and state laws.

Issue Number 2: Right Person, Wrong Seat

You may have inherited, hired, or promoted the Right Person who you've come to realize is in the Wrong Seat. Although they're a role model for your Core Values and fit your organization's culture, they're not producing.

And despite your Quarterly Conversations, they're not responding. This is a difficult issue and one where you're avoiding a decision because you genuinely like this person. Here are two examples:

- He has been with you through thick and thin, but he's in over his head and has become a bottleneck. He can't keep up with the volume and is stressed most of the time.
- Everyone loves her, but she isn't completing tasks on time and is struggling in her role. Others are picking up the slack and letting their own responsibilities slide.

This situation is especially tough when yours is a small organization. These people likely have been with you since the beginning, and you don't have another "seat" where the Right Person could fit. Assuming that you are a for-profit organization, you can't keep someone on your payroll just because you like them. Ideally, if your organization is large enough, you might have another seat. This solution happens often and should be your first choice. Here's a success story of moving someone to a more appropriate seat.

At Broder and Sachse Real Estate, Russell was sitting in the acquisition and development analyst seat, where he spent his days doing financial analysis. He was young and bright and shared the company's Core Values to a T. His manager, Lee, and coworkers loved him, and he wanted to stay with the company. But, the truth was he wasn't a very good analyst and he didn't particularly like it.

After a year of valiant efforts by both Russell and Lee to make it work, Lee had a tough conversation with Russell. He had to consider his options with Russell—someone who was an absolute fit in the company, just in the wrong seat. His first goal was to find Russell the right seat, because if there wasn't one, he'd have to go. Lee's gut told him that Russell was more of a people person and not a spreadsheet person. Fortunately, there was a position available in the property management department.

Upon making the change, Russell immediately excelled in the role. He became an instant superstar. His tenants loved him and he loved the job. This simple solution had a huge impact on the company, Russell, his manager, and his customers.

Yet you have to take a further step if there are no other seats available. How you handle this people issue speaks volumes about how much you care about your people. You've created awareness through your Quarterly Conversations and you've completed the Three Strikes. You're convinced that you've done everything you can to help, and you decide to let the person go. Here's how:

- Schedule a meeting at a time and place where you won't be interrupted. Follow your company's termination policy, and if it offers a severance package, have that and your documentation completed before the meeting.

- State the issue clearly and get to the point quickly: "Herb, despite our conversations about the need for you to step up and keep pace with the growing demands of your job, you've continued to struggle. The results just haven't been there. You've been a champion of our culture and I care about you personally. However, it's time we part company so you can pursue a job that's a better fit for you. I will help you as you search for the right opportunity. In the meantime, I've prepared a severance package for you to consider ..."

- Keep the rest of the conversation focused on answering questions that Herb might have about his severance and how you'll help him find the right opportunity elsewhere.

You've terminated Herb in a way that allows him to leave with dignity and to focus himself on his future. You've made the right decision for the greater good of your team—a decision that Herb will eventually acknowledge was difficult but necessary. Plus, you'll sleep better knowing that you did everything you could to help Herb while he worked for you and during his search for a job better suited to his skills.

We've had some bosses tell us that they've reached out to people in their network to help employees like Herb find employment quickly. They win because they get someone they care about into the right seat. Herb wins because he finds a new position that is a better match for his skills. They understand that people like Herb aren't "bad people"—they're just in the wrong seat.

Issue Number 3: Wrong Person, Right Seat

You may have inherited, hired, or promoted people who you've recognized and rewarded for exceptional production and output, only to hear rumblings that they are getting those results in ways that are damaging your company's reputation, aggravating fellow team members, and undermining everything that you're trying to accomplish for the long term. These are usually me-first versus we-first people who put their interests before the Core Values of the organization. In the meantime, they continue to produce results, but behave and get those results in ways that go against the company culture. In other words, while they are highly productive short term, they are killing your company long term.

When you ignore this issue, you're telling your organization that the Core Values that you espouse don't matter when compared to results. In describing these people, one boss stated, "Wrong people in the right seats are what we call 'productive jerks.' They're arrogant and painful to be around."

Do not let these people hold you hostage. Your reputation with your people and your customers is at stake. Here are three examples:

- You hired him for his technical knowledge to engineer a product that's due to launch in eighteen months. He lords his knowledge over people and refuses to share his expertise with others. His massive ego and arrogance make him difficult to work with, but you've avoided rocking the boat until after the new product reaches the market. Meanwhile, he's telling everyone that he should be running your department.

- You've awarded her Top Salesperson of the Year. She's crushing her numbers. You know she's not a team player but you tell yourself that hunting is rarely a team sport. You're also afraid that if you fire her, she'll take her customers with her. However, at a trade show your best customer tells you that she is abrasive and backstabbing. Your direct reports and peers give you specific examples of how she wins through intimidation. Still, you're having a tough year, and firing your top salesperson will make it even tougher.

- You have a customer service representative in your department that you inherited from your predecessor. She has been with the company since its founding. She's competent in her role but doesn't share a Core Value: "Do What It Takes." At times everyone in the department must put in extra time to fulfill a customer's need, but she is unwilling to go the extra mile to make it happen. She leaves right at five o'clock despite being in the middle of a major customer issue. This is harming the entire team because she's clearly viewed as someone unwilling to stretch as far as they do.

These are moments of truth for your Core Values. You must make them count. Unfortunately, people in this category are often blind to behaviors that undermine the culture. Or, they rationalize cynically that getting results is all that matters. You can imagine the damage they're doing to your organization, especially when they're rewarded for outstanding performance.

If your direct report's behavior hasn't changed despite your Quarterly Conversations and after applying two of the three strikes, they must go. But you must be prepared for how you handle this situation.

For example, you may have a deep concern that their departure will jeopardize the company because they might take key accounts and perhaps key employees with them. If this is the case, you must have a well-thought-out plan to minimize any exposure that the company might have. Some of our clients waited up to two years to make this difficult change because they needed that time to build a strong enough sales team around them, strengthen client relations, and generate enough revenue to be less vulnerable. As an example, you might arrange to contact every customer within twenty-four hours of the termination and meet with every employee.

You have scheduled the meeting to deliver the Third Strike. Here's how:

- Ensure that you and your boss are on the same page with the need to terminate the person's employment.

- If you have a human resources professional, ensure that they concur and that all documentation is completed.

- Schedule the meeting and follow your company's termination policy. If it includes a severance package, have it and your documentation completed before the meeting.

- Meet with the person, state the issue clearly, and get to the point quickly: "Curt, despite our conversations about the need for you to become more collaborative, willingly share information with others, and live by the Core Values, it's still obvious to me and the entire department that you haven't done so. The latest incident is just one more case in point. You withheld your analysis of customer purchase patterns, causing our department to miss a critical deadline for completing our sales plan. This is unacceptable and shows a total disregard for the goals that we set as a team. I've decided that it's time for us to sever our relationship."

This type of termination can be difficult, but the impact that it has on your organization's culture can be huge. In one of our sessions a boss shared that he had fired his top performer for blatant disregard of two Core Values. Within minutes of the termination employees knocked on his door, thanking him for firing the guy. Within days he was getting calls from old customers who wanted to reconnect.

Kelly Cuellar of Zoup! shares this story about the importance of making this tough decision, insisting that Core Values carry true weight:

"I had an employee who had just finished training in a management role. She had been very receptive during training and was performing to expectation. She was in her second month with the company, and we had begun the process of letting her take the reins. Two weeks into running her team solo, I began to hear unfavorable reports that she was not following proper processes, and how poorly she was speaking to her team. I quickly arranged a meeting and clarified our expectations that had been set on her first day. I reviewed with her our Core Values, and the importance of how we treat our people, and I put it in writing, which she also signed. At the end of the meeting, she stated she understood the expectations and she would achieve them. We agreed to meet again in thirty days.

"Two weeks later, we were still receiving complaints, had lost one of our great employees, and were about to lose a second. We could not wait the full thirty days to act. I had to terminate her. She was not surprised, and left within ten minutes without argument. It's unfortunate that sometimes an employee knows they are being let go, and they wait for it to happen. When it's a business-critical decision, you have to act. If you've given them the direction, you've given them notice, and they still aren't performing, you've done all you can. It's a 'don't care' scenario and you can't fix 'don't care.'"

Issue Number 4. Wrong Person, Wrong Seat

This issue is the most obvious and hopefully is discovered within the first ninety days of hiring someone or, if you inherited them, of your taking charge. If you've followed our strong recommendation in the previous chapter to keep the circles connected with a weekly Meeting Pulse, the deficiency will be glaring within weeks. Ignoring the issue has dire consequences, as shared by an employee who had this experience while working for a not-so-good boss:

"My boss had an employee in a critical position who was definitely the wrong person in the wrong seat, but he refused to deal with her. Despite being in her position for over two years, she did not understand the system-driven parts of her position and ended up making a lot of work for everyone else in our department. Part of the problem was that he hired her and did not want to admit that he had made a mistake. The other part was that he was one of those bosses who believe they can 'save' people and make them better. He was in fact destroying the morale of the entire department that caused some key employees to quit."

Equally distressing is when a boss believes that having anyone in the seat is better than having an empty seat. One boss summarized this belief well when he said, "Half an ass is better than no ass." This is actually a boss issue, not just an employee issue.

When you realize before, during, and after Quarterly Conversations and weekly meetings that the person is clearly below The Bar for Core Values and GWC and hasn't improved even after Two Strikes, you must let the person go. Follow the same procedure that we outlined in Issue Number 3.

Sometimes, however, the issue is so blatant, as in cases of stealing, fraud, and damage to company property, that you should skip Strikes One and Two and move directly to Strike Three and terminate the employee.

In all of these employee situations, you should realize that you must take the lead. Though termination may make you uncomfortable, it is also part of being a boss. It's unfortunate that in many companies, employee relations issues are thrown into the laps of the human resources department, putting them in the difficult situation of having to mediate every dispute. One company tasked their HR manager with terminating "bad employees." These terminations occurred on Fridays, which, as you might guess, became known throughout the company as "Black Friday." This practice led to a culture of fear.

You cannot abdicate your role as boss. When bosses fail to address employee issues personally and quickly, bad things happen. The worst blow is that you lose the respect of your people. They want to know that you care about them, their behavior, and their performance. HR should help bosses deal with employee issues in a consistent, fair, and timely manner—not do their work for them.

By addressing the Four People Issues head on, you will demonstrate that you have what it takes to be a great boss. Removing disruptions also counts when you are trying to breed a powerful culture with Great People.

CHAPTER 10

a final word on people

"Character is higher than intellect—a great soul will be strong to live, as well as strong to think."
—Ralph Waldo Emerson

AT THE BEGINNING OF THIS BOOK, we asked you to consider the fact that your people are your number one competitive advantage. Whether you've hired them or inherited them, you must take responsibility for them, because they are your most valuable resource. Ultimately, you are accountable for their performance or the lack thereof.

Great bosses succeed in getting the most out of their people. To ensure that success becomes a habit, they continually raise the expectations of their people and hold them accountable to higher standards. They get their people to bring their A games every day. They're willing to leave their office, to walk the shop floor and meet with people to see and hear firsthand what's happening. They invest time in their people, knowing that the opposite of success isn't always failure—more often it's complacency that leads to failure.

When you continually raise The Bar, a potential side effect is some turnover. You may be asking yourself, "Is this a good thing or bad thing?"

GOOD TURNOVER, BAD TURNOVER: A REALITY CHECK

When helping our clients become great bosses, occasionally, at about the one-year mark, the issue of turnover comes up. When it does, we clarify the issue by asking them, "Is it good turnover or bad turnover?" Upon further investigation, the conclusion is always on the positive side. Good turnover is people going away because they are the Wrong Person, they are in the Wrong Seat, or they can't live up to the new expectations. Bad turnover is when the Right People are leaving because of poor leadership and management. In other words, they're working for bad bosses who let bad people linger on.

Whenever your vision for growth is crystal clear, the right structure is in place to support that growth, and you push to get the Right People into the Right Seats—leading, managing, and holding them accountable to execute the vision—there will be fallout.

Anytime your company breaks through the ceiling and goes to the next level, it is going to experience some turnover. For most of our clients the average is about 20 percent in the first year. The most was 50 percent. It's also important to note that 80 percent of the time, the company's Leadership Team itself changes. Several of our clients have completely turned over their entire Leadership Team, where the only person left was the owner.

One boss reflected, "I should have acted faster to get Right People into the Right Seats! I replaced one-third of my Leadership Team over a two-year period. I knew the people I replaced were the wrong people earlier when I decided to rebuild the company. Getting it done faster would have given us a competitive edge sooner."

With all that said, it's undeniable that, intuitively, any kind of turnover doesn't feel good. However, think of the benefits when you replace the wrong people with the right people. You gain more of what you want from your business: productivity, growth, profit, enjoyment, peace of mind, and a thriving culture. At the same time, you greatly diminish the things that you don't want: frustration, dysfunction, politics, whining, and stagnation.

Having Great People throughout your entire organization is possible when you do the addition and subtraction necessary to make it happen.

At this point, you may be feeling that becoming a great boss is going to take a lot of work. The fact is, you are already doing a lot of work. Having mediocre people in place and having Great People in place take equal amounts of hard work, but as boss you get to choose which—enjoyable hard work or frustrating hard work. We urge you to choose enjoyable hard work. Set The Bar high, have clear expectations, repeat them often, and be willing to walk the talk.

Here's an image of what your ultimate job is as a boss. A vision is achieved more quickly when everyone's energy is focused on common goals. Imagine the people in your organization as arrows, each with goals, objectives, values, and energy. If people have conflicting goals, objectives, and values, then the arrows all point in different directions and energy is wasted. As a result, your organization is spinning its wheels, stuck or frustrated by its slow pace. It looks much like Diagram 19:

Diagram 19

Now imagine those arrows as people aligned with your organization's values and objectives. In this case, all of them are pointing in the same direction. Your organization or department moves forward freely and effortlessly, and together you achieve more. The combined power that's generated propels the team even faster. As the boss, you have the ability to make all of the arrows point in the same direction like Diagram 20:

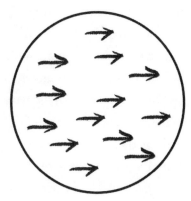

Diagram 20

This is ultimately your job—to get all the arrows pointed in the same direction. We've given you all the tools to do just that.

SUMMARY

We began this book by defining the title "boss" as a term of respect used to address a person in charge. Throughout this book we used the term "boss" purposely because that's what you are—someone in charge, who leads and manages people. We then shared the results of both the Gallup and Harris polls that revealed that most American workers are not engaged at work. At the heart of this epidemic are bad bosses.

In an effort to prevent this from happening in your company, we then took you on a journey to becoming a great boss. You can do that by learning and implementing some real-world, practical tools. We'd like to quickly recap those tools for you in this summary.

We first explained that when it comes to the role of being a great boss, you must Get It and genuinely Want It. From there we explained further that you must have the Capacity to do it, and then defined the four types of capacity to make sure you possess all of them. With all four types of capacity in place, we then showed you a simple tool, Delegate and Elevate, to help you identify the activities that you must delegate to consistently free up your time to be a great boss.

With that context clear, we then turned to your people and gave you a powerfully simple tool, The People Analyzer, to define Great People for your organization, and ultimately confirm they are all the Right People in the Right Seats, at or above The Bar. We then went to the heart of what makes great bosses, The Five Leadership Practices and The Five Management Practices. By employing all these practices with each of your direct reports, you'll be a great boss.

We completed a deep dive on the Quarterly Conversation to help you communicate better, stay connected to your people, and constantly improve your relationship. We identified the Four People Issues that you will likely face as a boss and shared specific ways to handle each one. We also shared the Three-Strike Rule as an effective method to deal with people who consistently fail to meet your expectations.

This handful of powerful tools will make you great. If you are feeling overwhelmed in any given area, applying the relevant tool will help you on your way to being a great boss. Choosing just one to begin with might also be a good starting point. But using all of the tools together has a powerful synergistic effect that will dramatically improve your skills, accelerate your results, and make you a great boss.

Here's a final story about what happens when great bosses get all the arrows pointing in the same direction, and how the power that's generated propels their team even faster.

During the 1936 Olympics, held in prewar Nazi Germany, nine determined young men from the University of Washington rowing crew climbed into their sixty-foot boat, the *Husky Clipper*. They had overcome seemingly insurmountable obstacles just to make it to the Olympic Games. Then they were placed purposely in the worst lane, one subjected to high winds and choppy waves. Yet after a grueling effort, they emerged victorious 2,000 meters later to capture the gold medal. They epitomized the meaning of the inspirational poster that hangs in so many conference rooms today: "Together we achieve more."

Those gold-medal-winning young men were chronicled in a book aptly named *The Boys in the Boat*. Author Daniel James Brown describes George Pocock, the man who designed and built the *Husky Clipper*, as someone who "learned to see hope where a boy thought there was no hope, to see skill where skill was obscured by ego or by anxiety. He observed the fragility of confidence and the redemptive power of trust. He detected the strength of the gossamer threads of affection that sometimes grew between a pair of young men or among a boatload of them striving honestly to do their best."

Coaching them was a quiet boss, Al Ulbrickson, who worked tirelessly to place the boys in seats that matched their abilities and strengths. He ensured that each one shared a common goal of becoming a champion and brought out the best in them. Ulbrickson and Pocock got it, wanted it, and had the capacity to help their young men overcome all obstacles to achieve the gold medal. They were great bosses.

We thank you, boss, for reading this book, and we hope our message has resonated with you. We hope you see that these tools and practices are simple and recognize that the journey is not easy. It takes continual practice to be a great boss.

Your journey of becoming a great boss now begins. Apply the tools that we've taught you. Come back to this guide regularly, and someday soon one of your direct reports, during a Quarterly Conversation, will smile and say, "You're the best boss I've ever worked for!"

Wear the title "boss" with pride. You've earned it!

TOOLS SUMMARY

1. **Delegate and Elevate™** (pages 25–27): The ultimate time-management tool and guide to focus on activities that harness your strengths and lead to a more effective and fulfilling workday.

2. **Core Values Exercise** (page 42): A method used by the Leadership Team to "discover" the attributes and characteristics of the people that your organization must have to consistently deliver value to your customers or clients.

3. **The People Analyzer™** (pages 43–48): The simplest, most effective way to assess whether you have direct reports that are aligned with your Core Values and that truly Get it, Want it, and have the Capacity to do what you need done.

4. **Quarterly State of the Company Agenda** (page 62): An effective meeting format to share your vision and keep your employees in the loop on where your organization has been, where it is, and where it is going.

5. **Clarity Break™** (pages 73–76): Time that you schedule away from the office, out of the daily grind, to think and to work *on* your business.

6. **The Leadership Self-Assessment** (page 77): A simple yes/no questionnaire to help you focus on the Five Leadership Practices that you must consistently do to become a better leader.

7. **Rocks** (pages 81–82): The most important priorities that you must accomplish in the next ninety days and a five-step process for how to establish them with your team.

8. **The Meeting Pulse™** (page 93): The agenda for an effective weekly meeting with your team (www. eosworldwide.com/level-10).

9. **The 5-5-5™** (page 98): Creating context with Core Values, Rocks, and Roles for a meaningful Quarterly Conversation centered on what's working and what's not working.

10. **The Three-Strike Rule** (pages 104–105): How to deal with direct reports when they consistently fail to meet your expectations.

11. **The Management Self-Assessment** (page 107): A simple yes/no questionnaire to help you focus on the Five Management Practices that you must consistently do to become a better manager.

12. **The Annual Review** (page 127): A form and method to recognize key accomplishments, acknowledge areas to improve, and devise a plan to make it happen and a forum for keeping expectations crystal clear.

ADDITIONAL RESOURCES

1. *Traction: Get a Grip on Your Business*, Gino Wickman, BenBella Books, 2011

2. *Get a Grip*, Gino Wickman & Mike Paton, BenBella Books, 2012

3. *Decide! The One Common Denominator of All Great Leaders*, Gino Wickman, Amazon Kindle Edition, 2009

4. *The One Minute Manager Meets the Monkey*, Ken Blanchard, William Oncken Jr., & Hal Burrows, Harper, 1989

5. *The Five Dysfunctions of a Team*, Patrick Lencioni, Jossey-Bass, 2002

6. *How: Why HOW We Do Anything Means Everything . . . in Business (and in Life)*, Dov Seidman, John Wiley & Sons, 2007

7. *Willful Blindness: Why We Ignore the Obvious at Our Peril*, Margaret Heffernan, Walker Books, 2012

8. *Crucial Conversations: Tools for Talking When Stakes Are High*, Kerry Patterson, Joseph Grenny, Ron McMillan, & Al Switzler, McGraw Hill, 2012

9. *The Progress Principle: Using Small Wins to Ignite Joy, Engagement, and Creativity at Work*, Teresa

Amabile & Steven Kramer, Harvard Business Review Press, 2011

10. *1501 Ways to Reward Employees*, Bob Nelson, Workman Pub. 2012

11. *Primal Leadership: Realizing the Power of Emotional Intelligence*, Daniel Goleman, Richard Boyatzis, & Annie McKee, Harvard Business Review Press, 2013

12. *Fierce Conversations: Achieving Success at Work & in Life, One Conversation at a Time*, Susan Scott, Berkeley, 2004

ACKNOWLEDGMENTS

This book would not have been possible without the help and guidance of the following people. We will never be able to thank you enough for your impact on our lives, our work, and this book.

Gino's Family and Friends

Kathy, my strong and beautiful wife. I could not do what I do without your support. I appreciate you and love you with all of my heart.

Alexis, my incredible daughter. You are as beautiful on the inside as you are on the outside. You make me so unbelievably proud and make me smile every day.

Gino, my quick-witted son. You are an engineer with a personality. Thank you for always making me laugh. I am so incredibly proud of you.

Linda Wickman, my mom. For your quiet strength, your wisdom, and your inspiration. You always make me feel so loved. I think about you every day and love you very much.

Floyd Wickman, my dad. You get all the credit for The People Analyzer, the discipline of criticizing in private and praising in public, and the two emotions exercise. Thank you for everything you taught me about leading and managing people; it changed my life. You are the entrepreneur's entrepreneur.

Sam Cupp, my business mentor. You get all of the credit for keeping the circles connected, and the powerful question, "Do you want to do what's best for the company or do you just want to do what you want to do?" Thank you for meeting with me every month for all of those years. You turned me into a businessman. Since your passing, there isn't a day that goes by that I don't miss you.

Karen Grooms, the world's greatest business manager. You keep me in my unique ability and protect me from the world. Thanks for over twenty years of holding all the pieces together.

René Boer, my coauthor. You are one of the most tenacious, funny, and passionate people I know. It has been a pleasure working with you on this project. Thanks for your commitment to the EOS cause and for being the example.

EOS Worldwide Leadership Team (Don Tinney, Mike Paton, Amber Baird, Lisa Hofmann, Tyler Smith, Ed Callahan, and Marisa Smith). Thank you for running the company like a Swiss watch so that I can continue to create content for the entrepreneurial world.

My Clients, for over 1,700 full-day sessions of enabling me to do what I love. Thank you for the risks you take, your passion, your incredible hard work, and the many lives you impact.

René's Family and Friends

Judy, my wife. Thank you for standing by me through thick and thin. You have a gift for listening, caring, and making everyone feel important. Life is an adventure made special with you by my side.

Allison and Erin, my daughters. I am proud of the beautiful and strong women that you have become. I love you for your inquisitive nature and empathy for others, and for creating the joy that surrounds you. Thank you for letting me take the scenic route.

My grandkids Whitney, Trent, Everett, and Maeve, who keep me on my toes. I love reading with you, playing with your toys, and watching you grow.

Mike and Ty—my two favorite son-in-laws. Thanks for being such great husbands, fathers, and all around handymen.

My mom and dad, Catherine and Jacob Boer, who emigrated here and inspired me and my brothers Andrew and Frank, and sisters Anita, Diane, and Mary, to pursue our dreams. I hope that we have made you proud of us.

James C. Suski, who lived his Five Rules for Life every day, inspiring his family, friends, and colleagues to be the best they can be. He made the years in his all-too-short life count.

Bill Ferril, for taking a risk and giving me an opportunity early in my career to help you build a great company. I will always appreciate your kindness and support.

Jim Murty, for encouraging and motivating me to meet your expectations. Thank you for setting a high standard. Shine on, my captain!

My clients, for trusting me to help them get the most from their people and their business. A special thank you to Jerry Thiel, my first EOS client, for letting me practice on you and your team!

Gino Wickman, one of the most positive, amazing, and humble people I have known. Thank you for creating the opening and letting me run with it. I am doing what I love to do, with people I love, making a difference and having fun along the way.

Contributors

Story Contributors: Chris Beltowski, Mary Boer, Dennis Burke, Kelly Cuellar, Rob Dube, John Eadie, Eric Ersher,

Dick Gill, Ben Goetz, Sue Hawkes, Debra Hutson, Mike Kotsis, Kris Marshall, Trevor Moses, Jan Mustian, Chris Naylor, Andrew Park, Paul Ruby, Todd Sacshe, and Anna Saville.

The Manuscript Readers: Kurt Adair, Amber Baird, Debra Behring, Chris Beltowski, Rich Bevis, Mary Boer, Jinney Brombeg, Dennis Burke, Kelly Cuellar, Hamsa Daher, Jon Dickinson, Rob Dube, Eric Ersher, Ben Goetz, Colin Hansen, Sue Hawkes, Lynn Herbert, Brad Hermann, Nicholas Heinton, Gretchen Hopp Doyle, William Kenyon, John Kohl, Mike Kotsis, Michael Lee, Kim Luebke, Kris Marshall, Trevor Moses, Jan Mustian, Chris Naylor, Sergio Pages, Curt Rager, Paul Ruby, Todd Sacshe, Nick Sarillo, Anna Saville, Daniel Sobiechowski, Kristy Swope, Anthony Walsh, Mark Willoughby, and Rick Wilson.

Other Contributors: Our editor, John Paine of John Paine Editorial Services; our literary agent, Matthew Carnicelli of Carnicelli Literary Services; Drew Robinson of Spork Design; Veronica Maddocks; our publisher, Glenn Yeffeth, and the team at BenBella Books—thank you for helping us tell our story to inspire and help bosses everywhere become truly great.

ABOUT THE AUTHORS

GINO WICKMAN's passion is helping people get what they want from their businesses. To fulfill that passion, Wickman created the Entrepreneurial Operating System® (EOS), a holistic system that, when implemented in an organization, helps leaders run better businesses, get better control, have better life balance, and gain more traction—with the entire organization advancing together as a healthy, functional, and cohesive team. Wickman spends most of his time as an EOS Implementer, working hands-on with the leadership teams of entrepreneurial companies to help them fully implement EOS in their organizations. He is the founder of EOS Worldwide, a growing organization of successful entrepreneurs from a variety of business backgrounds collaborating as certified EOS Implementers to help people throughout the world to experience all the organizational and personal benefits of implementing EOS. He also delivers workshops and keynote addresses.

RENÉ BOER has thirty years' restaurant industry experience with national brands such as Pizza Hut and Jamba Juice. He's been a franchisee, corporate executive, and small business owner. Since 2008, as a Certified Implementer of EOS, the Entrepreneurial Operating System, he has worked with

Leadership Teams at more than fifty privately held companies, helping hundreds of bosses grow their organizations while enjoying personal freedom.

A life-long cyclist, Boer helped create a unique cycling event, the Sub-5 Ride, which, since 2010, has raised more than $500,000 to support the mission of the Davis Phinney Foundation "to help those living with Parkinson's Disease to live better today."

Download the

HOW TO BE A
GREAT BOSS

Toolkit

**Get the tools you need to lead, manage, and hold
your team accountable:**

/ Evaluate how well your people fit your company culture
/ Determine whether everyone is in the right seat
/ Identify tasks and responsibilities to delegate
/ Assess your ability to lead and manage effectively
/ Uncover areas where you can improve
/ Communicate clear expectations to your team

Download the toolkit by visiting

HOWTOBEAGREATBOSSBOOK.COM

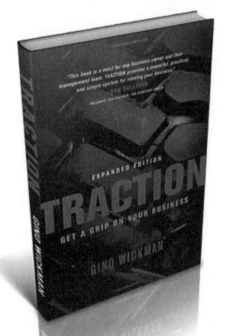

GET A GRIP

An Entrepreneurial Fable:
Your Journey to Get Real,
Get Simple, and Get Results

by Gino Wickman
and Mike Paton

ROCKET FUEL

Discover the vital relationship that
will take your company from
"What's next?" to "We have liftoff!"

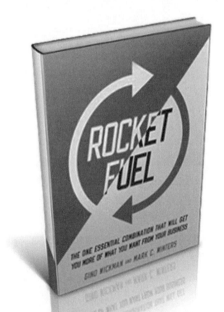

by Gino Wickman
and Mark C. Winters

Learn more at
eosworldwide.com/rocket-fuel

0144